Hal Schell's guide to
CRUISING
AND
HOUSEBOATING
THE DELTA

(Formerly: Guide To Houseboating The Delta)

*This book is dedicated to Joanie
who labored mightily to help
make it a reality*

Published by Schell Books
Copyright © 1982 by Hal Schell

Photography by the author

ISBN 0-9605322-3-4
*Original printing March 1978: 9,000 copies
Second printing July 1978: 5,000 copies
Third printing August 1979: 7,500 copies
Fourth printing April 1981: 8,500 copies
Fifth printing June 1982: 10,000 copies
This book is reviewed and updated at each printing*

Additional copies $4.95
plus 75 cents postage and handling
(Calif. residents add 30 cents sales tax)
**From: Schell Books, P.O. Box 9140, Stockton, CA 95208
VISA • Tel. (209) 951-7821 • MasterCard**

CONTENTS

Helpful Listings

1

Your Introduction To The Delta

The Delta's 1,000 miles of navigable waterways are an extraordinary enticement for anyone wearied by the hectic pace of modern-day city life. There is a sort of rural charm to the Delta. And it seems to have not yet been sullied by the trappings of civilization.

There is a sense of history to the place. You can gaze up at the towering Mount Diablo, visible from most all of the Delta, and visualize that cool March day in 1772 when Spaniards Pedro Fages and Fray Juan Crespi trekked to the top and cast their eyes on the Delta.

They were the first white men to do so. And to them it looked like a great inland lake. For the rivers, swollen by winter rains, had all overflowed their banks. It was an area rich with fish and game and was inhabited by some 30,000 Indians.

Later the white man came in greater numbers. Men of vision realized that the peat soil here was incredibly rich and they set about wresting it from the rivers. The first levees were constructed in the middle of the 19th century with the aid of Indian labor. They were crude affairs of stacked tule sod and didn't hold for long.

When the last spike was driven for the transcontinental railroad in 1869, it provided a windfall of sorts for the Delta. For it surplused a great force of Chinese laborers. They flocked to the Delta, putting their backs to the building of levees. They moved the soil to the levees for the meager sum of 13 cents per cubic yard.

Development of the clamshell dredge speeded up reclamation of the Delta. Its giant teeth could chomp into the river bottom mud and move it to the levees for the piddling sum of a nickel per yard and in the process it deepened the waterways and helped form the networks so

enjoyed by today's boaters.

By 1930 some 700,000 acres had been reclaimed forming 55 man-made islands. Reclamation of the Delta was considered complete. The harvests were bountiful. It seemed anything could grow in the rich Delta soil.

If you peer over the levees you will see vast fields of corn, asparagus, potatoes, sugar beets, tomatoes and other crops. Grape vineyards have recently done well. Orchards of pears, peaches and other fruits decorate the landscape along the Sacramento River.

Until machinery made them obsolete, large forces of workers were required to tend these crops. They were mostly foreigners and their ethnic ties even today are strongly felt. They lived and loved, worked and played in company towns that today have disappeared. The islands supported their own schools. One could spend months without ever leaving his island.

In everything that was done, the water had to be reckoned with. Homes were built on stilts with high second stories so that residents could scurry up to where it was dry during times of inundation. Children became accustomed to going to school by rowboat during times of high water.

The harvest was delivered to market by barges, scows, steamboats and just about anything else that would float. You can still see the rotting stubs of pilings that mark former landings where steamboats stopped at the farms for pickups and deliveries.

Later, when truck transportation became financially preferable, the trucks were ferried to and from the islands by crude cable-drawn ferries. Today, about a dozen of these still exist, going about their work much as they did many decades ago.

You can drive an auto aboard for a free ride to many Delta islands. For some, the ferries are the only access to the mainland.

The Paddlewheelers

No time period of the Delta strikes the imagination quite like the paddlewheeler era. They first came sloshing up the Sacramento River to deliver miners to the gold fields during the great gold rush. Then they stayed on to make regular runs to San Francisco from Stockton and Sacramento.

Estimates put the total of these fine old steam-powered boats at over 200 in the Delta. Sternwheelers outnumbered the sidewheelers at almost two to one, for they could better maneuver in the narrow channels. They carried both passengers and freight.

They travelled as far as Fresno on the San Joaquin River and Red Bluff on the Sacramento River. These were exciting times and there was fierce competition for passengers and freight. There were boiler-bursting races between steamboat captains. The more reckless of the breed would try to ram and sink a competitor's boat. Differences were oft times settled with pistols.

The *Delta King* and *Delta Queen*, each 250 feet long and capable of carrying 1000 passengers, were launched in 1927. For a decade or so, they were the pride of the fleet. But business began to deteriorate in the 1930s. Shortly before WW II they were retired from service. The *Queen* now plies the Ohio and Mississippi Rivers carrying passengers there as it once did here in the Delta.

The *Delta King* is another story. For years now it has existed in a legalistic briar patch. It has been slowly decaying in Stockton, then Sacrmento, then Collinsville then Rio Vista. After purchase at a bankruptcy auction a few years ago, it was hauled off to Richmond to be converted into a floating restaurant destined for the wharfs of San Francisco. It never happened. Half sunk now, there's a proposal to sell time-shared cabins in the boat and move it to the Maritime Museum in San Francisco. I'm not holding my breath waiting for this to happen.

Delta Geography

The Delta's borders are ambiguous. And perhaps this is appropriate. For the reigning attitude here is lackadaisical. What difference does it make where the Delta actually begins and ends? But if you must have limits, on a map draw straight lines from Pittsburg to Tracy to Stockton to a spot midway between

The old Fort Sutter churning down the Stockton Channel, heavy with passengers. Its dying days were spent as the "Poop-Deck Gun Club".

Courtland and Sacramento and back to Pittsburg and you'll have it pretty much contained.

Uh, now that we know what and where it is, what do we call it? *The Delta* is what all us river rats prefer. *California Delta* is in some favor because it makes for a neater package. *San Joaquin-Sacramento Delta* (with names reversed according to where you live) is more accurate. *Sacramento Delta* is very bad, for it both mislocates the Delta and underplays the major portion of it that exists around the San Joaquin River.

The Delta boasts three major rivers—the San Joaquin, Sacramento and Mokelumne (pronounced mu-col'-umne with the first u soft). The San Joaquin is "houseboatable" from where it joins the Stockton Deepwater Channel and below. With caution, you can cruise above this junction if you can clear the bridges.

The Sacramento is okay all the way to the capitol city, but offers no route variation after Sutter Slough joins it just below Courtland. Most rental houseboats are not permitted below the Antioch bridge on the San Joaquin.

The Mokelumne splits off into two forks that both offer fine cruising. Its upper portion above New Hope is fine until the juncture of the Cosumnes below the bridge. The Calaveras River below Stockton is good for a short run to about the bridge at Interstate 5.

The Water Life

Six days each week Lou Sparrenberger, the River Route postman makes his assigned 65-mile run in a fast runabout delivering mail to island residents.

The sheriffs of the five Delta counties and one or two cities keep the peace patrolling in a flotilla totalling over two dozen vessels.

A regular morning task for children living on many islands is to crank up the outboard motor and splash in to catch the school bus at a designated rendezvous.

When the Lost Isle propane supply dwindles, a propane truck from Campora Gas Services drives over a swing bridge, bounces onto a cable-drawn ferry, drives along a narrow dirt levee road to trundle onto a rickety diesel-driven barge that

transports it close enough to the Isle to dispense its precious fuel.

Huge ocean-going freighters from faraway places like Russia and Japan share the waters with fishermen in tiny rowboats while on the way to the ports of Stockton and Sacramento.

Life in the Delta is predominately water oriented. The work boats make room for the pleasure fleet, which at times measures way up into the tens-of-thousands. They somehow amicably coexist with hot skiboats, lumbering houseboats, big wake-producing yachts, tacking sailboats and humble cartop fishing boats.

Hang around long enough and you will see it all in the Delta. Sea planes drop in for landings, sharing docks with boaters. Kiters glide high in the air, trailing behind

Lads at the Boathouse In Locke do this "poor man's Acapulco" for passing cruise ships.

their tow boats. Crop dusters fly a whisker width above the fields. Daring youngsters make great sport of precariously dangling from lines trailing from flapping spinnakers.

Four Season Fun

In no way are activities on the Delta limited to just the warm summer months. The fall can be exquisite with long strings of balmy days. September-October are the favored months of many boaters.

The fall stripped bass run begins in September, attracting droves of anglers for this fine fish that can go to over 60 pounds. The Delta is on the route of the western flyway and offers some of the best duck hunting to be found. The arrival in the Delta of the snow geese is an exquisite sight. They land in rice paddies by the thousands, creating a cacophony of sounds heard for miles.

Winters on the Delta are crisp and bright, with plenty of sunny days. Boaters seek out sheltered areas where they can bask in the sun and keep their tans intact. Tule fog some days is a fact of winter life here however, and will keep boaters in port. Although usually it will burn off by mid-morning.

Spring signals the return of boaters who have mothballed their vessels for the winter. Yacht clubs stage opening day parades and festivities. There is another striped bass run. Boaters reckon with windy days by seeking out a favored sheltered cove.

Summer gets busy, starting about mid-June. Days are hot but with cool comfortable evenings. Visiting boats from the San Francisco area spend endless weeks here. The rental houseboat fleet is out in full force. The throaty skiboats, with their glistening chrome engines, are on the move. Favored anchorages are spilling over with people having fun. The summer is carnival time in the Delta.

Yet the so-called "off season" can be more satisfying. There's more time to get to know one another. And that is part of what the Delta is all about.

Why The Houseboat

I doubt that anyone just set about to invent the houseboat. More likely it was an idea that just went its own logical course. And the Delta was the most logical place for it to happen.

For years, cruisers have been the most popular Delta boats. They have the "boaty" look about them. They are designed to handle rough water. But the basic design of the cruiser V-hull limited interior liveability considering the length and beam (width) of the boat.

It became evident that boaters who never left the amiable waters of the Delta were not putting their cruisers to their full designed-for use—yet they were saddled with the craft's limitations. A roomier, less-expensive boat seemed more appropriate.

The houseboat evolved. The most popular was the pontoon or catamaran houseboat. It could easily be made with a wide beam that provided plenty of interior livability. They were powered with relatively inexpensive and easy to maintain outboard motors. Interiors incorporated all the desirable features of a compact apartment—running water, toilets and showers, kitchens (galleys) with sinks, plenty of counter space and iceboxes or refrigerators. They had comfortable sleeping for six or more persons.

Because they did not look "boaty" enough, they were not very popular with some of the cruiser people. But slowly a second kind of houseboat evolved. It had a broad hull, was often inboard/outdrive powered and combined features of both the cruiser and the houseboat. It too became popular.

Today the houseboats vary from the outboard-powered catamaran to a few hulled styles capable of rough water duty, with many types in between. It is not so much a question of which is best as it is to personal preference and cost.

George Ladd started the first Delta houseboat rental business back in 1961. He built his boats in his Stockton boatyard and they have always had a reputation for quality and ruggedness.

No one knows for sure how many houseboats are dawdling around the Delta today. I'd guess the number to be in excess of 3,000. They have become a distinctive part of the Delta. And you see them everywhere.

Perry Mason author, the late Erle Stanley Gardner, was a Delta houseboating buff and he spent the last seven years of his life here. At one time his personal houseboat fleet consisted of five! All on the Delta.

11

2

Renting A Houseboat

Little did Stockton boat builder George Ladd realize what he was starting when he placed a modest advertisement for his Delta rental houseboats in *Sunset Magazine* back in the early 1960s. The ad attracted the attention of the publication's editorial staff. And some of them decided to give Delta houseboating a whirl.

They meandered around the Delta for a week in one of Ladd's houseboats, then trudged back to their typewriters to tell the world about it. Their adventures were featured in the March 1963 issue.

"All hell broke loose after that," says George Ladd. "We were inundated with inquiries from all over, 40 to 50 a day." Callers were interested both in buying and renting houseboats.

Ladd couldn't build new houseboats fast enough to keep up with the demand. The modest little 24-foot rentals he began with gave way to increasingly larger boats, eventually both 36- and 40-footers.

Competition began to proliferate. Eventually a fleet of some 300 rental houseboats was available on the Delta. One firm alone boasted 120 rental houseboats. But other firms were casual operations with only two or three boats.

The cost of operating and maintaining a rental fleet kept rising. The marginal operators dropped by the wayside. The business matured. Today there are a dozen or more Delta houseboat rental firms with a total of perhaps 200 houseboats.

None are what you would think of as "big business." This means you can expect warm, friendly, personal service. Yet even a modest size rental fleet represents a sizeable investment. So they all have to operate in a businesslike manner. Their terms are clear and their equipment as advertised.

What a remarkable variety of houseboats is to be found in that 200-plus houseboat fleet. There are sleek hulled boats of fiberglass or steel, inboard-powered and some with flying bridges.

There are specially built catamaran type boats with raised wheel houses and powered by twin outboards.

There are rugged pontoon boats of heavy gauge aluminum or steel. Most of these are single outboard powered, but a few of them have inboards.

"What type would you recommend?" I am so often asked. Invariably my replies are couched in ambiguous terms. For most any of these boats will serve quite nicely on a Delta houseboating holiday. Each type comes with its own advantages and disadvantages. Some offer more amentities than others. But you very often pay more for these too.

The inboard/outboard-powered (I/O) hulled boats have more of the "boaty" look about them. They are capable of faster speeds, but usually their engines are governed so you won't damage them by over revving. The nature of Delta houseboating is supposed to be lazy cruising. Most of the rental boats will perk along at 10 mph or better and that's plenty fast enough. It lets you absorb the scenery en route. And it will give you fuel consumption in the order of 2½ to 5 gallons per hour.

Each rental outfit will gladly send you brochures that provide details on the boats they offer. They'll contain floor plans and equipment lists so you'll know exactly what you are renting. They'll answer your questions on the phone. If you live close enough to drop by, they will let you examine their boats if any are in port.

Six- or 8-sleeper boats are the most

commonplace. But some will sleep 10 and a few firms include boats to 50 feet in their fleet. Interior arrangements vary on different make boats. Generally the dinette converts to a fairly narrow double bed. Divans will pull out to make roomy double beds that still may be somewhat smaller than your double bed at home. Some boats also have over and under single-person bunks.

If anyone in your party is over-sized, it is a good idea to have a close look at bed sizes to be sure they are adequate. In the summer months, children often prefer the "adventure" of retiring in sleeping bags on the decks outside.

Two or more couples or families often double up on a houseboat rental so they can share costs and enjoy the outing together. Most houseboats will partition into at least two separate staterooms for a measure of privacy.

Sharing costs can make a houseboating vacation quite inexpensive. Especially when you consider that you are getting both your hotel and transportation in one exciting package.

But the confines of a houseboat over a long period can bring out both the best and worst in a person. Know your friends well before you agree to spend a week or more aboard with them. Frequent stops that let everyone get off the boat for some private time ashore help.

No Experience Needed?

Can it be true? A landlubber with absolutely no boating experience whatsoever can plunk himself behind the wheel of a multi-ton 40-some-foot behemoth of a houseboat and in an hour or so be a skipper of great skill?

Well, yes—and no. Yes, the rental operator will be able to teach you enough during the orientation and shakedown cruise so that you will adequately be able to cruise with the boat, get it next to and away from docks, anchor it and in general have a very good time in it. No, you will not yet be an expert skipper.

There is a learning period during which you will get a feel for what it is all about. The longer you use the boat, the better you'll get at handling it. Advice tendered in the next two chapters will quicken the learning process if you study it in advance.

Every year some 3,000 tyro skippers take over the helm of Delta rental houseboats. And they are living, breathing proof that it can be done. Consider too, that a vast number of new and used houseboats sold annually are purchased by eager land dwellers with little or no boating experience.

No one is born with boating experience. It is acquired. Incidently, your orientation will include hands-on practice with you at the wheel of the boat you are renting. This may take an hour or so. So don't expect to push off within a few minutes after being introduced to your houseboat.

Reservations

Almost all Delta houseboats are rented by reservations. You normally don't amble in off the street and rent a boat on the spot. The summer months, especially between mid-June and Labor Day, are popular and may book eons in advance. If you dally over making reservations, you are apt to be disappointed.

Yet there are exceptions to this rule. A last-minute cancellation might free up a boat. If on short notice you decide you want to go houseboating, it can't hurt to call a few rental operators to see if a boat is available. And there are instances when you can just walk in off the street without a reservation and within an hour be off cruising down some tranquil Delta slough.

Don't plan on it, however. Reservations are the name of the game.

During the peak season, many firms specify a minimum rental period—usually a week. This is understandable, for the turn-around time when a boat has to be cleaned and prepared for the next customer can eat into the time it is available for rental.

But not all firms have this rule. And some are flexible enough so they will rent you a boat for an in-season weekend if one is available. You'll never know unless you ask.

Deposit And Insurance

A reservation deposit is normally required and it is held as security on the return of a clean, undamaged boat. If you

14

Above. Kids and pets love the boating experience. L. Some outfits supply a dinghy with your rental.

cancel within a specified period, which varies somewhat from one firm to the next, then all or most of the deposit is returned. This protects the firm against last-minute cancellations that do not allow them enough time to rent the boat to someone else.

I honestly feel that none of these operators really want to keep the deposit from an excusable late cancellation. And they will usually move mountains to try to accommodate you in some other way. Most often they try to schedule you for another date.

The rental price of the boat normally includes deductible insurance. The deductible amount may vary somewhat between firms, and may or *may not* apply to both damage your boat incurs and damage it might do to other boats or property. It is a good idea to be quite clear in advance on the terms of your rental insurance.

You'll sign off on an inventory list of the goodies that came with your boat. Naturally, if you lose an anchor or a deck chair or a dinghy or whatever, you'll be expected to pay for it.

Most operators start you off with a new or reconditioned propeller. They will point out to your how free of nicks its blades are. And they will advise you that if you return it bent and battered, you will be charged a reconditioning fee.

Dinged props are one of the minor hazards of boating on the Delta. While under way the skipper needs to keep a wily eye out for floating logs, pilings and other hazards. He moves cautiously in shallow water and stays away from rocky shores. He is especially careful when backing up, for that is when the prop is most vulnerable.

I am out on the Delta water every week, covering many miles. A couple of years ago I damaged two props in three months but haven't dinged once since. So chances are good that you'll not damage a prop on your rental. But if you should, smile, pay the modest reconditioning fee and consider yourself a member of the gang.

Kids and Pets

Children go bananas over the adventure of houseboating. Swimming. Dangling a line over the side for catfish. Exploring an island "jungle." And they are welcome by all rental outfits. Houseboating is considered very much a family experience.

Houseboats are outfitted with at least enough life jackets for everyone aboard. But if you have small children, check to see that there are enough life jackets in children's sizes. Boats with wide walk-arounds and railings will be safer for the kids.

Most rental outfits also welcome "reasonable" pets. Your favorite ocelot or herd of St. Bernards would probably not be deemed reasonable. Dogs adapt well to houseboating. But taking Fido for a walk when your boat is anchored away from shore can present a problem. A dinghy is handy for this transportation chore. Check with your rental operator to see if one is supplied or if you may rent one separately. Marinas where you stop require that pets be on a leash.

Off Season Discounts

I take objection to the term "off season." For spring and fall are some of the Delta's finest seasons. They are anything but "off." Be that as it may, tantalizing discounts of 20 percent or more prevail starting sometime in September and extending to mid-May or longer. Some operators offer even better discounts for the winter season.

There is no problem renting a houseboat for just a weekend during the off season, although reservations are still recommended. If you live within an easy drive of the Delta, you can monitor winter

weather. And if it looks to be good, make a last minute rental reservation for a weekend and join the rest of us winter river rats.

A houseboating "weekend" usually begins around 6 p.m. Friday and ends 6 p.m. Sunday, with some variations. At least one firm offers inexpensive weekday off-season packages.

Reasons To Houseboat

As if you needed reasons. But all too many people associate renting a houseboat solely with the big vacation. While most any occasion will suffice as an excuse to go houseboating.

My two sons have birthdays just four days apart in late October. Years ago I rented a houseboat for a weekend and let each of them invite a couple pals along for a weekend floating birthday party. Needless to say, it was a success.

Newlyweds like to take houseboating honeymoons (some even get married aboard) and all the ingredients are there. Quiet anchorages for being alone. Boat-in restaurants for dining and dancing. Stunning days for skimming over the water on skis.

Holidays aboard are great. Most houseboats have ovens or barbecues and you can cook the bird aboard for an outstanding Thanksgiving, Christmas or Easter repast. Check the oven size carefully in advance to make sure your bird will fit. An 11 pound, 6 ounce turkey just squeezes into my boat oven. A 12-pounder would never make it!

Business meetings. Executives have found that the atmosphere aboard a houseboat is perfect for a weekend business meeting and that much gets accomplished.

Hunting. Duck hunting in the Delta is outstanding and millions of ducks migrate here annually. But most of the islands are owned by farmers or duck clubs. Without influence, your chances on hunting ashore are slim.

But you *can* anchor a houseboat along side a duck-club island, turn off the motor and get some very good shooting from the boat. One rental operator even provides camouflage netting for the houseboat!

Water skiing. Water skiers tire of the

Happiness is exploring the Delta by houseboat.

long commute home trailering the boat after a day's skiing. The Delta has some of the best skiing to be found anywhere. More and more water skiers are renting a houseboat and towing their ski boats along. It makes a fine comfortable base. It lets them explore new Delta skiing waters that otherwise might have been too far away for a round trip from their launching ramp. Expect fuel consumption on a houseboat to be somewhat higher when you are towing a boat.

Fishing. Fishermen are stoic souls, seemingly content to sit out in a small boat and shiver from the cold, but always in anticipation that a big one will take the bait. Some are learning that it is preferrable to fish from a comfortable warm houseboat that has all the amenities of home. The fish don't know the difference.

Breakdowns

Occasional breakdowns are a fact of boating even on the best rental houseboats and on the more superbly maintained owner boats. They are nothing to fret over. Your houseboating philosophy should, however, make allowance for the possibility of a breakdown in which your boat may be immobilized for a few hours.

If you are at a marina when the problem occurs, then there will be things to do ashore while you wait for the rental operator's mechanic to come to the rescue. If you are anchored out in the water, then just sit back and enjoy the quietude.

If the boat breaks down while you are under way, very quickly get an anchor placed so current or wind will not take you to shore and possibly damage the boat. If your boat is outfitted with a radio, then call the rental operator for help.

If not, then stop the first passing boat. Give him the name and phone number of the rental firm, your name and the boat number, and try to explain the nature of the problem. Ask him to call the rental outfit. If you feel you are in danger, ask that the Coast Guard also be called. It is a good idea to stop more than one boat so you will be sure of getting the message through.

For help during the day, stand up high on the boat and wave your arms up and down from the side of your body or wave a large white cloth. If you merely wave a hand, other boaters are apt to just think you are friendly. If stranded at night, wave a flashlight or lantern.

Even with 1,000 miles of waterways, the Delta is surprisingly compact. A mechanic's chase boat can get to you most anywhere in an hour or so. You will see boating traffic in the Delta's most remote sectors. Just relax. Have fun.

Things To Bring

Rental boats have everything you need to set up housekeeping including dishes, silverware, pots, pans and portable or built-in barbecues—but not bedding (with exceptions) or personal things like hand soap and towels. You need to bring your own sheets, blankets, pillows and pillow cases. Many find it easier to use sleeping bags.

Your clothing selection will depend on the season, but even in the summer should include a windbreaker or sweat shirt to ward off the cool of some nights. Dress is pretty casual. You'll be welcome most anywhere if your garb includes shoes and shirt. Waterside laundromats are listed in case you require one.

Food stores and restaurants are not

scarce on the Delta, but they may not always be convenient to where you are. So meals that can be coaxed out of cans are handy to have along. If you are faced with a long auto drive to the start, check to see if you can buy bread, milk, eggs and a few other perishables at or near the marina. Always keep your ice supply topped off.

Steaks, hot dogs and hamburgers are fun to barbecue and will keep longer if you start out with them frozen. Use this book's grocery store listing to plan cruises that include stops to replenish supplies.

It's a dead certainty that you will bring more supplies and equipment than needed. We all do. And the excess stuff just gets in the way. A vacation is for fun, so don't over worry about what to bring. You can probably buy what you forget. And if all else fails, maybe you can borrow that needed cup of sugar from the boat anchored next door.

Things To Bring For Your Houseboating Vacation

1. Two pairs of tennis shoes (or any soft rubber-soled shoes with treads). Leather soled or heeled shoes are frowned upon.
2. Bathing suit (2, if you want to swim and sun bathe).
3. A sweat shirt (sometimes it gets a mite cool in the morning or evening).
4. A warm jacket comes in handy when the cool air comes off the water.
5. A warm pair of pants is equally handy.
6. Underwear, several sets. Sometimes you're not close to a laundry.
7. Socks, several pair.
8. Sun tan lotion and sun burn lotion.
9. First aid kit (for nicks and scrapes).
10. Camera, film, and flash bulbs.
11. Sun glasses. The sun can really glare off the water. Binoculars.
12. A hat to keep the harsh sun rays off your dome.
13. One dress-up outfit in case you plan a trip ashore to go to dinner, etc.
14. Two pairs of shorts or cut-offs.
15. Sleeveless and sleeved shirts (I would take 3, 2 without, 1 with).
16. Books and magazines (catch up on your reading).
17. A portable radio to keep you up to date on the latest news and music.
18. Fishing tackle and fishing license.
19. Coleman lantern. Flashlight.
20. Mosquito repellent.
21. Air mattresses (it's fun to float after you've been swimming awhile).
22. Soap and cleaning agents.
23. Paper towels.
24. Paper plates, cups, and glasses (it's nice to not have to always wash dishes).
25. A cooler to keep your canned drinks iced down in.
26. Toilet tissue.

Groceries And Odds N' Ends

a. Canned meats—most are good hot or cold. I've found Spam, corned beef hash, and canned bacon really helpful.
b. Dinty Moore stew is a favorite.
c. Pork n' beans.
d. Any canned spaghetti products.
e. Vegetables.
f. Cereals individual dry packs are easiest.
g. Instant potatoes and rice.
h. Dry milk to use in potatoes, coffee, etc.
i. Salt, pepper, sugar, and flour (for frying fish).
j. Cooking oil and mayonnaise.
k. Sandwich makings (bread, lunch meat).
l. Snack items (cheese, crackers, chips, dips, salami).
m. Coffee or tea or maybe hot chocolate.
n. Charcoal and starter fluid.
o. Matches.
p. Milk, eggs, bread, and butter. These can also be bought at many cafes on the Delta, if you run short.
q. Ice (start out with a good supply and add to it as it melts).
r. Eight track tapes (if your boat has a tape deck).
s. Canned soft drinks, and Kool-Aid for emergencies.
t. Cigarettes.
u. Beer, liquor, and mixes. Take-out beer is available everywhere, but take-out liquor stores are scarce.

21

The Delta will bring out the Huck Finn in most anyone. These youngsters are having a time on Steamboat Slough.

23

ON-THE-WATER FACILITIES
PITTSBURG TO AMERICAN RIVER

RESORTS AND BOAT HARBORS	MAP LOCATION	TELEPHONE NUMBERS	SKI-BOATS	HOUSEBOATS	FISHING BOATS	BOAT LAUNCHING	BOAT & MOTOR REPAIR	DRY DOCK	PUMP-OUT STATION	CAMP & RV SITES #	SITES W/ELECT. #	SITES W/WATER. #	SITES W/SEWER. #	SHOWERS	RESTROOMS	LARGE CRAFT	SMALL CRAFT	ELECTRICITY	OVERNIGHT	RESTROOMS	SHOWERS	GAS & OIL	DIESEL	LAUNDROMAT	ICE	PROPANE	BAIT & TACKLE	MARINE SUPPLIES	GROCERIES	SNACK BAR	RESTAURANT	TAKE-OUT LIQUOR	COCKTAIL LOUNGE	BEER BAR	DAY CLOSED
ANDREAS COVE	D-5	(916) 777-6409								30						•	•	•	•	•					•		•			•				•	W
B & G BOATS	G-6	(209) 462-3976			•																			•				•							
B & W RESORT MARINA	D-5	(916) 777-6161				•										•	•	•	•	•	•			•			•	•			•	•		•	
BEACON HARBOR	I-2	(415) 684-2174																						•		•									T
BEAN POT RESORT	D-3	(916) 777-6550														•	•									•				•		•			
BETHEL HARBOR	I-2	(415) 684-2141			•	•				30	30	30		•	•	•	•	•	•	•	•			•		•	•	•	•	•					
BIG BREAK MARINA	F-3	(415) 757-5501		•	•	•	•										•	•	•	•	•	•		•		•						•	•		M
BLUE HERON HARBOR	D-4	(916) 777-6172		•						48	48	48	48	•	•	•	•	•	•	•	•			•		•		•		•	•	•	•		
BOATHOUSE IN LOCKE	B-6	(916) 776-1204		•	•	•										•	•	•	•	•				•		•		•			•	•			
BOB'S MARINA	J-2	(415) 684-2388																						•											T
BOYD'S HARBOR	I-2	(415) 684-2105			•					8	8	8		•	•	•	•	•	•	•				•		•		•	•	•	•		•		
BRANNAN ISLAND STATE REC. AREA	D-3	(916) 777-6671			•	•		•		•				•	•																				
BULLFROG LANDING & MARINA	F-6	(209) 465-9610		•												•	•			•				•			•	•	•	•					
CAMP-A-FLOAT	E-6	(209) 951-7518	•																					•											
CAROL'S HARBOR	J-2	(415) 684-2803		•	•	•										•	•	•	•	•	•			•		•		•			•	•	•		
CHANGING TIDES	H-8	(209) 982-0765								10	3	3		•	•	•	•	•	•					•		•		•			•				
CHART ROOM MARINA	A-2	(916) 371-0471			•	•										•	•	•	•	•	•			•		•				•					
CLIFF HOUSE	C-4	(916) 777-5375														•	•	•	•	•											•				
CLIFF'S MARINA	C-2	(916) 665-1611				•										•	•	•	•	•	•			•		•	•	•			•		•	•	
COLLINSVILLE RESORT	E-1	(707) 374-2521			•					30	30	30		•	•	•	•	•	•	•	•			•		•	•	•		•	•	•	•		
COURTLAND DOCKS	A-5	(916) 775-1360		•												•	•	•	•	•	•			•		•		•			•	•	•		
CRUISER HAVEN	G-5	(415) 634-3822														•	•	•	•	•	•			•		•					•				
DECKHANDS SUPPLY	B-6	(916) 776-1370			•	•		•								•	•	•	•	•	•			•		•		•			•				
DEL'S BOAT HARBOR	H-5	(209) 835-8365		•	•											•		•	•	•	•			•		•		•			•		•		
DELTA ADVENTURES	I-2	(415) 684-2884	•																					•											
DELTA COUNTRY HOUSEBOATS	B-6	(916) 776-1741	•	•		•	•	•																•											
DELTA MARINA YACHT HARBOR	C-3	(707) 374-2315			•	•	•	•	•	20	20	20	20	•	•	•	•	•	•	•	•	•	•	•	•	•		•			•	•	•		
DELTA RESORT	I-3	(415) 684-2122			•					75	20	20		•	•	•			•	•	•	•		•		•		•		•		•			
DELTA SPORTSMAN	J-2	(415) 684-2260			•																			•		•		•	•	•					
DELTA VAN CRUISER	J-1	(415) 684-2770	•																					•											
DISCOVERY BAY YACHT HARBOR	G-4	(415) 634-5928		•			•									•	•	•	•	•	•			•		•	•	•			•		•		
DOC'S MARINA	J-2	(415) 684-2327		•						10	10	10	10	•	•									•		•	•								T/W
DRIFTWOOD MARINA	E-3	(415) 757-9449			•											•	•	•	•	•	•			•		•									T/W
EDDO'S BOAT HARBOR	E-3	(415) 757-5314		•	•	•				35	35	6			•	•	•	•	•	•	•			•		•	•	•		•	•				
ERNIE'S	C-4	(916) 777-6510														•	•	•	•	•	•			•		•	•	•			•	•	•	•	
FARRAR PARK HARBOR	J-2	(415) 684-2352			•	•																		•		•				•					
FOUR SEASONS MARINA	B-2	(916) 371-6685				•										•	•	•	•	•	•	•		•		•		•	•		•	•		•	M
FRANK'S MARINA	I-3	(415) 684-3477								20	5	5	5	•	•	•	•	•	•	•	•			•		•					•		•	•	
FREEPORT MARINA	C-2	(916) 665-1555								4						•	•	•	•	•	•			•		•	•	•	•	•	•	•	•	•	M
GIUSTI'S	B-6	(916) 776-1808				•										•	•	•	•	•	•			•		•					•	•	•	•	M
GOLDEN GATE ISLAND RESORT	B-4	(916) 775-9016		•						40						•	•	•	•	•	•			•		•				•		•		•	
HAP'S BAIT	C-3	(707) 374-2372														•	•	•						•											
HAPPY HARBOR	D-5	(916) 777-6575								6	6	6		•	•	•	•	•	•	•	•			•		•		•		•		•			
HAVEN ACRES	H-8	(209) 982-9979		•		•																		•		•		•	•		•	•		•	
HEINBOCKLE HARBOR	I-7	(209) 835-1050		•																				•		•		•	•		•	•			
HENNIS MARINA	J-1	(415) 684-3333		•		•	•			5	5	5	5	•	•	•	•	•	•	•	•			•		•	•				•				
HERMAN & HELEN'S MARINA	E-6	(209) 951-4634	•	•	•	•	•		•							•	•	•	•	•	•	•		•		•	•	•	•	•	•	•		•	M
HIDDEN HARBOR	C-4	(916) 775-1313														•	•	•	•	•	•			•		•	•	•		•	•			•	M
HOLIDAY FLOTELS	E-7	(209) 477-9544	•	•	•	•																		•		•	•	•							
HOLLAND RIVERSIDE MARINA	F-5	(415) 684-3667			•	•										•	•	•	•	•	•			•		•	•	•							
THE ISLAND	D-4	(916) 777-6084														•	•	•	•	•	•			•		•									
ISLANDS MARINA	A-4	(916) 775-1123			•					50				•	•	•	•	•	•	•	•			•		•	•	•		•	•		•		
KING ISLAND MARINE SALES	E-7	(209) 478-3377			•											•	•	•	•	•	•			•				•							
KING ISLAND RESORT	E-7	(209) 478-0210	•	•			•									•	•	•	•	•	•			•		•	•	•			•		•		
KO-KET RESORT	B-5	(916) 776-1488			•					15	15	15	15	•	•	•	•	•	•	•	•			•		•				•		•			M
KORTH'S PIRATES LAIR	D-5	(916) 777-6464		•	•											•	•	•	•	•	•			•		•		•			•				
LADD'S STOCKTON MARINA	F-8	(209) 477-9521				•	•									•	•	•	•	•	•			•				•							
LADD'S STOCKTON YACHT SALES	F-8	(209) 951-7572														•	•	•						•		•									SU
LAURITZEN YACHT HARBOR	E-3	(415) 757-1916		•		•	•									•	•	•	•	•	•	•		•		•	•	•		•	•		•		
LAZY DAYS HOUSEBOATS	J-2	(415) 684-3641	•																					•											
LAZY M MARINA	H-5	(415) 634-6259			•					50	50	50	50		•	•	•	•	•	•				•		•	•	•		•	•		•		
LEISURE LANDING MARINA	I-1	(415) 684-2166														•	•	•	•	•	•	•		•		•				•		•			T

RESORTS AND BOAT HARBORS	MAP LOCATION	TELEPHONE NUMBERS	SKI-BOATS	HOUSEBOATS	FISHING BOATS	BOAT LAUNCHING	BOAT & MOTOR REPAIR	DRY DOCK	PUMP-OUT STATION	CAMP & R.V. SITES #	SITES W/ELECT. #	SITES W/WATER. #	SITES W/SEWER. #	SHOWERS	RESTROOMS	LARGE CRAFT	SMALL CRAFT	ELECTRICITY	OVERNIGHT	RESTROOMS	SHOWERS	GAS & OIL	DIESEL	LAUNDROMAT	ICE	PROPANE	BAIT & TACKLE	MARINE SUPPLIES	GROCERIES	SNACK BAR	RESTAURANT	TAKE-OUT LIQUOR	COCKTAIL LOUNGE	BEER BAR	DAY CLOSED
LIGHT 29 MARINA	C-2	(916) 428-6280														•	•	•	•															•	M
LIGHTHOUSE RESORT	D-5	(916) 777-6681		•	•					100	85	85	75	•	•	•	•		•	•	•	•	•		•	•	•			•	•			
LLOYD'S HOLIDAY HARBOR	E-2	(415) 757-2346		•	•																		•			•				•				W
LOST ISLE	F-7	(209) 465-6649								75				•	•	•	•	•	•	•	•				•					•	•		•	•
MARINE EMPORIUM	J-2	(415) 684-2330		•	•											•	•						•		•	•	•	•	•				•	
MIDDLE RIVER INN	G-6	(209) 465-8412												•	•								•							•	•		•	
MOORE'S RIVERBOAT	D-5	(916) 777-6545			•									•	•	•	•														•	•	•	•
MOSSDALE MARINA	I-9	(209) 982-0512								14				•	•	•	•						•							•	•			
MOSSDALE TRAILER PARK	I-9	(209) 982-0358		•						11	6	11		•	•	•			•	•			•		•	•				•	•			
MOZZETTI MARINE	I-2	(415) 684-3216		•	•																														
NEW BRIDGE MARINA	E-2	(415) 757-1500												•	•	•	•	•	•		•	•	•		•		•	•	•				•	
NEW HOPE LANDING	B-6	(209) 794-2627	•	•	•					30	30	30		•	•	•	•	•	•		•	•			•	•	•	•	•	•			•	
ORWOOD RESORT	G-4	(415) 634-2550		•	•					50				•	•	•	•				•	•			•	•	•		•	•			•	
OUTRIGGER MARINA	D-3	(916) 777-6480			•					25				•	•	•	•	•	•	•	•	•	•	•	•	•	•	•	•	•	•		•	•
OX BOW MARINA	C-5	(916) 777-6060			•									•	•	•	•	•	•	•	•	•	•		•	•	•	•	•			•	•	
PARADISE POINT MARINA	E-7	(209) 952-1000	•	•	•	•	•	•						•	•	•	•	•	•	•	•	•	•		•	•	•	•	•	•		•	•	•
PERRY'S BOAT HARBOR	D-5	(916) 777-6461			•	•	•	•						•	•	•	•	•	•	•	•	•	•		•	•	•	•	•	•			•	
PILOT HOUSE BOAT HARBOR	B-2	(916) 392-7697			•									•	•	•	•				•	•	•		•		•	•	•				•	
POINT RESTAURANT	C-3	(707) 374-5400												•	•	•	•													•	•	•	•	M
RALEY'S LANDING	A-2	(916) 371-7700												•	•	•	•		•				•						•				•	
RANCHO MARINA	D-5	(916) 777-6135		•	•					50	50	50	25	•	•	•	•		•	•	•	•	•		•	•	•	•	•	•			•	W
RICHARD'S YACHT CENTER	J-2	(415) 684-2363			•									•	•	•	•				•	•				•	•							
RIVER GALLEY	A-2	(916) 372-0300												•	•	•	•												•	•			•	
RIVERSIDE INN & MARINA	C-5	(916) 777-6796				•								•	•	•	•	•	•	•	•	•	•		•				•	•		•	•	
RIVER VIEW MARINA	A-2	(916) 925-4100	•											•	•	•	•		•				•						•	•			•	
RIVER VIEW RESORT	I-3	(415) 684-2395								2	2	2	2	•	•	•	•												•	•			•	
RODGERS POINT MARINA	E-2	(415) 757-0270												•	•	•	•	•	•	•		•	•		•		•	•	•	•			•	Y
RUSSO'S MARINA	I-2	(415) 684-2024			•					20	12	12		•	•	•	•				•	•			•	•	•	•	•	•			•	
RYDE HOTEL	B-5	(916) 776-1318												•	•	•	•													•	•		•	
S & H BOAT YARD	E-3	(415) 757-3621	•			•	•	•						•	•	•	•																	
SACRAMENTO BOAT HARBOR	B-2	(916) 449-5712			•		•							•	•	•	•		•			•				•			•					
SAM'S HARBOR	J-2	(415) 684-2115			•					6				•	•	•	•	•	•				•		•		•		•				•	
SAN JOAQUIN YACHT HARBOR	E-2	(415) 757-9883												•	•																			
SHERMAN LAKE HARBOR	E-2	NO PHONE												•	•	•	•		•				•					•	•					
SHERWOOD HARBOR	B-2	(916) 371-3471			•					50				•	•	•	•		•				•		•	•	•			•			•	
SID'S HOLIDAY HARBOR	C-4	(916) 777-6351												•	•	•	•						•						•	•			•	M
SNUG HARBOR	C-4	(916) 775-1455			•					65	5	5		•	•	•	•		•	•		•	•		•	•	•	•	•	•	•		•	•
SPINDRIFT MARINA	D-4	(916) 777-6041												•	•	•	•	•	•			•	•		•	•	•	•	•	•			•	
SPOT, THE	D-3	(916) 777-6602								18	10	10	10	•	•	•	•	•					•		•	•	•	•	•	•	•		•	•
STEAMBOAT LANDING	A-5	(916) 775-1121												•	•	•	•		•				•					•	•	•	•		•	•
STEPHENS ANCHORAGE	F-8	(209) 951-4144												•	•	•	•	•	•	•	•	•	•		•		•				•			
SUGAR BARGE MARINA	I-2	(415) 684-3652			•					100		5		•	•	•	•	•	•				•		•		•		•	•			•	
TIKI LAGUN RESORT	F-6	(209) 941-8975			•					60	14	14		•	•	•	•	•	•	•	•				•	•	•		•	•	•		•	•
TOWER PARK MARINA	D-6	(209) 369-1041		•	•	•	•			250	157	157	157	•	•	•	•	•	•	•	•	•	•	•	•	•	•	•	•	•	•	•	•	•
TRACY OASIS MARINA	H-6	(209) 835-3182		•	•	•				35				•	•	•	•	•	•	•		•		•	•	•	•	•	•	•	•	•		•	
TUNNEL TRAILER PARK	B-5	(916) 776-1859								15	15	15	15	•	•	•	•	•					•		•		•		•	•				
TURNER CUT RESORT	F-6	(209) 946-9409								30	10	30	10	•	•	•	•	•	•		•	•	•		•	•	•		•	•	•		•	•
TURTLE BEACH RESORT	I-9	(209) 239-2034		•	•					220	35	35		•	•	•	•						•		•	•	•		•	•	•			•
UNCLE BOBBIE'S	E-7	(209) 477-4145			•									•	•	•	•												•	•	•			
UNION POINT RESORT	G-6	(209) 948-4294												•	•	•	•																	
VIEIRA'S RESORT	C-4	(916) 777-6661		•	•					65	47	47	24	•	•	•	•		•	•	•				•	•	•			•	•		•	•
VIEW POINT MARINA	A-2	(916) 372-3720		•	•	•	•							•	•	•	•		•				•					•	•	•			•	
VIKING HARBOR	J-1	(415) 684-2020												•	•	•	•												•	•			•	
VILLAGE MARINA	A-2	(916) 922-7548			•									•	•	•	•		•				•				•	•	•	•			•	
VILLAGE WEST MARINA	F-8	(209) 951-1551			•	•	•							•	•	•	•	•	•	•	•	•	•		•	•	•	•	•	•	•		•	•
WALNUT GROVE MARINA	B-6	(916) 776-1181	•	•	•	•	•	•						•	•	•	•	•	•	•	•	•	•		•	•	•		•	•	•		•	•
WALNUT GROVE MERCH. DOCK	B-6	NO PHONE												•	•	•	•						•				•		•	•				
WATERFRONT YACHT HARB.	F-9	(209) 943-1848				•								•	•	•	•						•		•				•				•	
WHISKEY SLOUGH HARBOR	G-7	(209) 464-3931		•	•					30	3		10	•	•	•	•	•			•		•		•	•	•			•	•		•	
WILLOW BERM BOAT HARBOR	D-5	(916) 777-6313												•	•	•	•	•	•				•			•	•						•	
WIMPY'S MARINA	B-6	(209) 794-2544			•									•	•	•	•		•				•				•	•	•	•			•	
WINDMILL COVE	F-7	(209) 948-6995			•					40	6			•	•	•	•	•	•	•	•		•		•	•	•			•	•		•	•

25

3

Docking And Un-Docking

When I took up houseboating in the Delta, I marveled over how helpful fellow boaters were. Whenever they saw me approaching a dock in my houseboat, they would scramble out to lend me a hand. Later I came to know that these were not totally altruistic acts. It seems these helpful skippers were trying to protect their own boats from damage my heavy 34-footer was capable of wreaking upon them.

Much of the skill required to handle a houseboat is called upon in the relatively routine acts of docking and un-docking. Yet the basics are straight forward. Anyone can do it if he gives some thought to the task at hand.

The number one rule is to go *ever so slow, ever so slow*. You merely want to *whisper* the boat up close to the dock. In a slow-moving boat, even if your docking plans should go slightly awry, you don't damage much more than your ego. A boat approaching the dock at any speed over a "crawl" advertises a novice at the helm.

The 4 most important words in this book are—*go ever so slow*.

You Steer With Your Rear

You are steering your houseboat from up forward not unlike in a car. In forward gear you turn the wheel in the direction you want the bow (front) to go and in reverse you turn it the way you wish the stern (rear) to go. From here on though, what happens is not one whit a la automobile.

Actually, you are turning the direction the entire motor on an outboard powered houseboat, and the direction of the outdrive portion of an inboard/outboard (I/O) equipped boat. The propeller then pushes the *stern* of the boat in the direction

required. And it pulls the *stern* when in reverse. Thus, the motor must be running, with the prop in gear, or you have no steering.

Think of how your car would behave if its rear wheels were the pair turning right and left with the steering. Many a tyro houseboater has staged a magnificent show up at the helm, steering first to the right, then to the left, oblivious to all but what lies straight ahead. Meanwhile, the stern has been doing its own version of the snake dance, arcing wide and narrowly missing everything from tree stumps to $50,000 yachts!

On a boat, it is the *stern* that does the turning. It will swing wide if you let it. You have to keep a wily eye on it, especially when leaving a dock. Your planned maneuvers must always consider its swing.

No Brakes For Stopping

Unlike a car, a boat has no brakes. The only way you can halt a boat's forward motion is by shifting into reverse. But a houseboat represents a lot of mass on the move. Propellers in reverse have less efficiency. You have to allow a lot of time for the reverse stopping action to take effect.

The procedure for stopping is to shift into neutral, center the wheel, then shift into reverse and apply throttle. It is important to center the steering wheel. If you don't do this, the reverse will also be turning the stern in whatever direction the wheel was turned.

Some boats have indicator dials that tell you when the steering is centered. Others will have a mark or tape on the wheel to help you tell when steering is centered. When maneuvering some outboard-powered houseboats in tight

26

quarters, it is convenient to have the rear door open so you can glance back at the engine and know when it is centered.

Effects Of Wind And Current

Both wind and current can influence the handling of your boat, and they are forces that must be reckoned with when maneuvering in close quarters. The force of the current varies in different parts of the Delta. Its direction changes and strength varies with the twice-daily tides. At some times and places there is no perceptible current action at all.

Delta winds are most often slight in the summer, but don't depend on it. The side of a houseboat presents a formidable obstruction to a brisk wind. Most Delta boaters seek out protected anchorages or harbors when the wind is blowing hard.

Old buffalo hunters would sight their rifles allowing for "windage" and so must you on occasion when sighting for a houseboat landing. You have to estimate what the wind action is doing to the boat, then allow for it.

Whenever humanly possible, you want to approach the dock against the wind and current. If you aren't certain of their direction, while out in the open, shift into neutral and note which way your boat drifts. You want to maneuver then with the bow opposite that direction. By approaching the dock against the wind or current, you retain maximum control. You apply just enough forward power to overcome wind or current force and "inch" in toward the dock. Should you get above this speed, then shift to neutral for a few seconds till wind or current slows you. Then shift back into forward.

On the other hand, if you approach a dock in the *same* direction of say a 4 mph current, then its speed will *add* to the forward speed developed by the motor. And you'd find it difficult to stop in time. So, always take the time to determine the direction of current and wind. And *approach against it.*

Some final words on the subject. Current and wind are not necessarily your enemies. Their forces can be used to your advantage to make it easier to dock and un-dock, as you'll see later in this chapter.

No Heroes Needed

Docking is never a time for heriocs. A good skipper always gets to the dock the easiest and safest way he can. He selects the roomiest portion of the dock available. If there are willing hands around the dock to help, he rejoices and takes advantage of them.

He gives a few toots on the horn well in advance of approaching the dock. This will often garner help from other boaters and maybe summon the harbormaster or dock hands. You can be a good boater first time out.

Plan Ahead

Have boat poles handy in case they might be needed. Position any rubber fenders required to keep your boat from scratching on the dock or on other boats. Have someone in your party (we call 'em deckhands) positioned on the forward "corner" of your boat that will make initial contact with the dock.

He should have an untangled line ready that is tied to the appropriate part of the boat—many a deckhand has jauntily hopped onto the dock with line in hand only to discover it is not tied to the boat, which by then is drifting merrily away! He should step to the dock, hold the boat slightly off, then make fast the bow line.

Virtually all Delta docks are the floating type. That is, they float on Styrofoam and rise and lower with the tides. Most are affixed to stationary wood pilings on which they slide up and down. Always tie to the dock. Should you tie to a piling, tidal action could damage your boat or the dock.

Practice Makes Perfect

It is not one whit demeaning for you to practice docking and other maneuvers, whether you be a first-timer out with a rental boat or a grizzled owner bent on honing your skills.

Choose an untrafficed spot out in the open. Mentally construct a dock there. Determine tide and wind effects. Then have a go at a few good "dockings". See how long it takes reverse to stop you when you are going faster than a "crawl". Try some sharp turns and observe the wide swing of the boat's stern. Try "docking" with the current direction to see how much trickier it is. You'll gain a better feel for your boat.

DOCKING

#1 *With wind or current ahead, off the dock, or none at all, approach the dock ever so slow at a 45° angle beginning approximately 4 boat lengths away.*

Shift to neutral till the current almost halts forward speed, then shift back into forward. As you get closer, rock back and forth from forward to neutral to keep the boat just inching ahead.

Have a deckhand ready with a tied line at forward dockside corner of the boat. About 5 ft. from dock, shift to neutral, center the wheel, then shift into reverse to stop boat just short of the dock. Deckhand should quickly hop to dock and tie the bow securely.

Do not turn off engine. Wind or current should bring the stern in. If not, turn the wheel toward the dock, shift into reverse idle and let prop slowly bring in stern. Tie off the stern. Then, and only then, turn off engine.

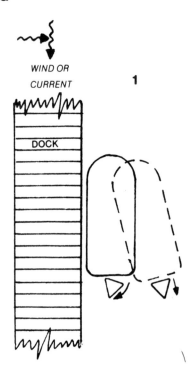

WIND OR
CURRENT

1

DOCK

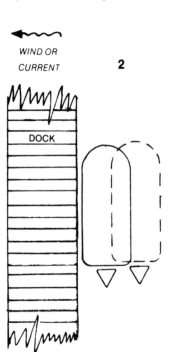

WIND OR
CURRENT

2

DOCK

#2 *With wind or current toward dock, proceed ever so slow parallel to and several feet off the dock. Position deckhands forward and aft on dockside of boat.*

Shift to neutral and halt forward motion. Let the wind or current take the boat to dock. Tie down bow and stern.

#3 If you have no other choice but to approach a dock with wind or current astern, well in advance position boat so it is parallel to and several feet off the dock.

While well in the clear, quickly center wheel and shift into reverse. See if reverse power is sufficient to overcome current or wind. If it is, keep steady reverse power, slacking off just enough to let boat inch forward. When opposite dock, apply enough reverse power to halt the boat.

With power still on, turn wheel all the way toward dock and let reverse prop pull the boat in. Have deckhand alert to immediately tie stern to dock. Then the current or wind will bring bow to dock.

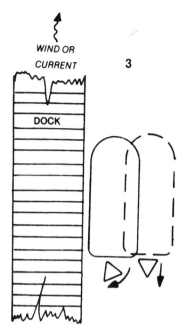

WIND OR CURRENT

3

DOCK

Un-Docking

Grizzled houseboaters prefer to leave a dock the easiest and simplest way possible. Often you can improve your undocking situation at crowded docks by moving your boat somewhat by hand. Say for example, you want to leave by going forward. But there's a boat tied too close to your bow to allow it. Yet there's plenty of room astern. Then while the motor is warming, simply get a couple deckhands to untie the boat and "walk" it back to the more desirable spot.

Other times, if politely asked, the skipper of a boat in your way will himself walk it (offer to help) to a spot out of your way if there is room to do so. Sometimes using a boat pole to push off will give you the extra couple of feet clearance you need to handily get away from the dock without incident.

These days many Delta marinas have harbormasters or dock hands, part of whose job it is to help you arrive at and exit their docks. Enlist help if it is crowded and you need it.

Un-Docking

(A) Bow-first departure with no wind or current, or wind or current from ahead.

Recall that the stern swings when turning. So you can't just turn the wheel away from dock and depart in forward or the stern will hit the dock.

Warm up the motor. Untie the stern. Have a deckhand untie the bow and give it a hefty push from the dock as he climbs aboard.

Be sure wheel is centered and proceed forward slowly. Don't turn the wheel until stern is well clear of the dock and all other boats.

WIND OR CURRENT

A

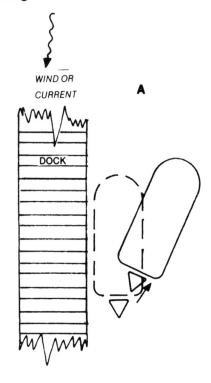

WIND OR CURRENT

B

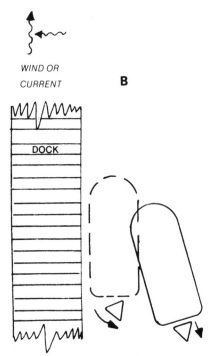

(B) Stern-first departure with no wind or current, or wind or current from astern or toward dock.

Untie the bow. Have a deckhand untie the stern and give it a hefty push from dock as he climbs aboard.

Turn wheel all the way away from the dock. Shift into reverse and back slowly away.

After stern is clear of dock, center the wheel and continue to back until bow is well clear of dock and any other boats. Then proceed as desired.

Note. If strong wind or current holds boat against the dock, proceed as in (D).

(C)   Wind and current off the dock.

Have deckhands untie both lines, then simultaneously push off bow and stern as they climb aboard.

*Remain in neutral till wind and current take the boat well clear of dock and any other boats. Then proceed as **desired**.*

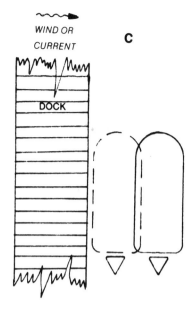

DOCK

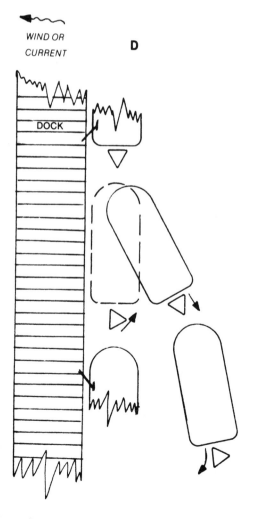

WIND OR
CURRENT

D

DOCK

(D)   Departure with strong wind or current toward the dock.

Or when boats are docked close both forward and aft.

Untie stern and bow. Turn the wheel all the way toward the dock. Shift into forward at idle speed.

The bow will nudge the dock and the stern will be pushed away from dock by the more efficient forward turning prop.

On some boats, a deckhand may have to hold bow of boat at dock by hand or with a line looped around a cleat. On fiberglass hulls, rig a fender between dock and boat to prevent scratches.

When stern is well clear, shift into neutral, center wheel, shift into reverse and back straight away.

Caution! Get well out into clear before proceeding so strong wind won't blow boat back.

Stern-In

Many Delta masrinas have stern-in parking rules so their docks will accommodate more boats. It doesn't mean you must park stern-to, but rather that you park end-wise or perpendi-cular to the dock. Virtually all houseboats are more comfortable with the bow to the dock. Sterning in can damage outboard motors and outdrives.

You can bring the boat straight bow-first to the dock, or sideways as per the appropriate #1, #2 or #3, to be wrestled into place by hand at your leisure. Stern-in marinas usually have dock help available, for they like to keep boats close together so there is room to entice new-comers. Tie the boat down snugly with lines off each "corner" of the bow. On fiberglass hulled boats, rig fenders between the bow and dock prevent scratching.

Crowded Stern-In Dock

Bringing a big houseboat bow-in to a tight vacated spot at a dock crowded with "stern-in" boats is no job for the faint hearted. I hesitate to recommend it to all but the most expert.

But if you must . . . First, make sure your boat will fit! Check wind or current drift carefully and try to approach against it. Enlist dockside help (blow horn, shout) from the two boats adjacent to the vacancy. Rig plenty of fenders on each side of the boat.

Be ever so thrifty with the throttle. Have deckhands on each side of the bow with lines. When you get close to the spot, have them throw the lines to adjacent boat helpers. The boat can then be moved into place by hand without help from the motor.

Getting Out

This is much easier. Have the wheel centered and "inch" out, alternating between reverse idle and neutral until the bow is well clear of adjacent boats. Then proceed as desired.

33

4

The Fine Art Of Anchoring

Anchoring out is perhaps the ultimate in the Delta houseboating experience. In an increasingly hectic world rife with rules and regulations, it is comforting to know that in the Delta you can still play the nomad and pick and choose where you want to stay for the day or a night— or even longer. Your choice of anchorage places is endless. They can be as peaceful and private as you care to make them.

But you best become acquainted with your anchors and the few perils involved in using them. I am reminded of a houseboating friend named Alex. He is the epitome of a fastidious houseboater. There is never a hint of dirt or grime on his handsome 42-foot hulled houseboat. It sports protective plastic runners over the companionway carpets so they won't be sullied by the dirty feet of mere mortals. And Alex prides himself on his boat-handling prowess.

Our boat club was having an impromptu raft-up at an anchorage on Latham Slough across from the hulk of a burned-out barge that has long resided there. The place is known for its deep water and hungry catfish. Alex arrived, unfastened his spotless anchor and gingerly pitched it overboard. We all watched as the anchor's expensive woven line payed out. It kept going and going— then the line disappeared.

Old salt Alex had neglected to tie the other end of the anchor line to the boat! He spent the remainder of the day trying to fish for an anchor rather than catfish. He met with no success. Oh, if I had but a nickel for every anchor that rests in the Delta bottom mud, I could retire.

The obvious lesson is to check your anchor lines to make certain they are securely tied to the boat. Then check 'em again before you toss out those expensive anchors. Too, always keep the lines untangled and neatly coiled. Should you have engine or propeller trouble, you want to be able to immediately throw out an anchor to prevent wind or current from forcing your disabled boat onto shore and possible damaging trouble.

Choosing Your Anchorage

Generally you want a spot off main routes heavily trafficked by boats. The place should be wide enough so that your boat is not in the least blocking the waterway. Best bet is to select a sheltered spot behind a levee bank or where there are trees or brush that will block the wind. The prevailing Delta wind is westerly, so the eastern side of an island will usually be preferable. Always anchor with the bow into the wind and pointed toward shore.

Meet Your Amiable Anchors

The most common anchor in use in the Delta is the Danforth type. It has light weight coupled with good holding power. But its pair of pointed "flukes" must become imbedded into the bottom mud or sand to hold. And the minimum amount of anchor line out must be 3 or 4 times as long as the water depth. If the line is too short (say 20 feet with anchor in 12 feet of water) the boat will lift the anchor because it tugs on it at too high an angle. When anchoring next to shore you will use both a stern and a bow anchor.

Anchoring Procedure

Approach the shore ever so slow with the boat perpendicular to the bank. Position a deck hand at the stern with anchor ready. Work out a signal with your deckhand such as a toot of the horn, a shouted word etc. You may want to open a window or the back door so he can hear you better. About 2½ boat lengths from shore, signal him to drop anchor. He should pitch it clear of the boat and at an angle so it is not near the motor or outdrive.

Now inch in toward shore while your deckhand pays out anchor line and makes sure it doesn't get near the prop. Inch in right up to the shore and have someone go ashore and secure the bow anchor around a tree or bush or by solidly imbedding the flukes into the river bank.

Next, hand-pull the boat away from the bank with the stern anchor line. Use the 8 foot boat pole to check the water depth off the forward portion of the bow. You want a high-tide clearance of at least 6 feet so you won't be aground at low tide. Pull the boat out until you have this clearance. Then take up the slack on both anchor lines and tie them down to the boat.

If, when you pulled on the stern anchor you found it was not holding, then pull it aboard. Leave the bow anchor ashore and ease off on its line as you slowly back out to again place the stern anchor.

Back out nearly the length of the bow anchor line, shifting into momentary forward to halt the boat and then into neutral. Drop the anchor off again. With the motor still in neutral, hand-pull the boat back toward shore with the bow anchor line. Again, pull on the stern anchor to make sure it is holding. It is of utmost importance that this anchor hold. If you must, repeat this ritual until the anchor holds.

Anchor Lights

When you are anchored out in the Delta, you are required to have the boat's 360-degree white anchor light on from dusk till dawn. It is not required when the boat is tied at a marina dock.

High And Dry

A good skipper checks his anchor lines from time to time and always before retiring for the night. It is important too to be sure there is always adequate water depth under the bow. A surprising number of boaters don't check for this. And in the morning they find the outgoing tide has left them high and dry. This provides great amusement for passing boaters. But it makes the skipper and crew feel sorta silly. And it assures that they will be in this spot for some time to come.

The boat motor is not up to the task of pulling loose a grounded bow, so don't try. Occasionally though, when the bow is just barely aground and you have a few muscled deckhands to lift and push the boat, you can back it off the sand. Get as much weight as possible onto the boat stern, then turn the wheel all the way in one direction and back the boat off one forward "corner" at a time.

On the other hand, if you anchor at low tide in the comfortable shade of the branches of a low overhanging tree, you are apt to wake in the morning to find tree limbs poking through the skin of your houseboat! A tide that rises as much as 6 ft. lifts your boat with it. And you want to make sure it has overhead clearance room to do so.

Don't Beach The Boat

The low tides uncover enticing sandy beaches just about anywhere in the Delta you are apt to be cruising. It is invigorating to break the routine of a cruise by anchoring up to one for an hour or two. The crew can go for a swim. Children can work off some of their excess energy. It is the perfect time for a picnic ashore.

So you can conveniently wade back and forth from boat to shore, you are

This angler hooked an anchor left by some hapless soul.

tempted to drive the bow right up on the beach. *But don't*. First, it is not good for most boats to have any part of the bottom touching. Second, you may have to wait for hours for another tide to release the boat.

But if you are watchful, you can depart somewhat from normal anchoring procedure and come up close enough to just keep the bow comfortably floating. You will have to regularly push the boat out a foot or so farther while adjusting the bow anchor. Give the bow enough water to spare so that the wake from a passing boat won't wash it ashore.

Anchoring In The Open

Occasionally you may wish to anchor out in the open, perhaps to fish or to swim off the boat in deep water. Then it is only necessary to set the bow anchor and let its line out the entire length. It is usually preferable to move to a protected anchorage before nightfall.

Anchoring Boats Together

In boating parlance, this is called "rafting up". And it is fun to be out where you can enjoy friends but still have the privacy of your own boat. The first boat should anchor so that there is room down stream for the additional boats to anchor. Make sure the anchors are set on each boat before the next is anchored in.

Carefully place rubber fenders off the bow and stern side rails to prevent damage from boats rubbing against each other during wave or wake action. You have to use common sense here, for the sides of different make boats often don't match well. I don't think it possible to rig too many fenders. Next tie the boats together using both forward and aft side cleats or the bottom portions of the railings.

Our boat club has had as many as 20 boats thus rafted. And it is always interesting to watch the juggling after one in the middle decides to leave early.

Weighing Anchor

Leaving the anchorage, that is. First, check to make sure you left nothing behind on shore—trash, deck chairs, tie-lines, coolers, pets, etc. Actually, this is good procedure anytime you make a stop. I can recall a boating pal of mine named Conrad Barrus shouting and waving his arms to me as he brought his big boat into the dock of one of the local Delta haunts. It seems that he just discovered that he'd left his revered pet dachshund behind at the last fuel stop. We had to hop into my fast runabout and make a speedy K-9 rescue.

Got everything? Okay, then start the engine and let it warm up in neutral. Loosen both anchor lines—but don't untie them from the boat! Hand pull the boat up to shore and have someone retrieve the bow anchor. Have him clean it before bringing it aboard and then neatly coil the anchor line. Now pull the boat back to the stern anchor, coiling the line as you go. When the line is straight up and down over the anchor, give it a hefty pull using both hands. Usually the anchor will come loose. Dip it up and down in the water several times to clean it.

If after several strong pulls you fail to dislodge the anchor, have a deckhand hold the line taut out over the side of the boat and well clear of the motor or outdrive. Manuever the boat so the *bow* is pointed *away* from the shoreline and is a few feet past the anchor. Tie the anchor line into a cleat or the bottom of a solid railing. Proceed in forward gear at a very low throttle to flip the anchor over and free it. Shift to neutral to stop the prop, clean and stow the anchor, and be on your way.

Keep Lines Away From The Prop

In an instant the prop can chomp through your anchor line. You've not only probably lost an anchor, but you'll have to untangle the remainder of the line from the prop. On an outboard, you can raise the engine to do this. On an I/O this may mean someone has to go into the water or try to accomplish this from the dinghy—or a service call. So deckhands need to take great care to keep anchor lines away from the prop. Likewise, when you leave a dock make sure no tie lines are left trailing in the water.

A giant raftup of Grand Banks trawler owners near Disappointment Slough. This annual affair takes place in July.

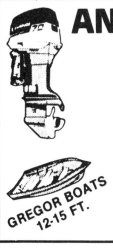

38

Tides N' Tules

In the Delta, the tide is not some sort of soap with which to do your laundry. The effects of the Pacific Ocean's tides are felt throughout the Delta. They provide a sort of flushing action to the Delta. And they assure that water depths are consistently deep even during times of drought.

But the amiable tide can leave you boat high and dry if you don't consider it when achoring.

What is the tide? Well, it's the alternate rise and fall of the ocean's water and the waters immediately connected to it. It occurs twice in a lunar day (24 hours, 51 minutes), that is 2 high and 2 low tides. It is caused by the attraction of the sun and moon. It varies in magnitude with the alignment of the two and the condition of the moon.

Because of that lunar day, high and low tides don't occur at the same time from one day to the next. Tide tables, published for each year, chart these high and lows. Many locally sold tables reference San Francisco, and include corrections for various areas including the Delta. Some are published with Delta corrections and these are easiest to use.

Normal Delta tides are in the order of 4 feet or so. But extreme "plus" and "minus" tides can go to over 6 feet and even to 9 feet in extreme cases. The "ebb" tide is the flowing back of the tide as the water returns to the ocean. The "flood" tide is the inflow of the ocean's water.

Although a boater should be aware of the tide, it is not anything to worry about. The tides lend character to the Delta and are kinda handy to have around.

Tules N' Peat

You can't hang around the Delta for long without hearing about tules and peat. They are related. The dictionary defines the tule as, "Either of two large bulrushes found in California and adjacent regions in inundated lands and marshes." Tules are everywhere in the Delta.

Peat is defined as, "Highly organic soil more than 50 percent combustible, composed of partially decayed vegetable matter found in marshy or damp regions."

It is the decayed tule that has formed the peat which makes the soil on the Delta farms so incredibly rich. Because it is combustible, there is summer fire danger on some peat islands. Peat fires can smoulder underground for days. And there are stories of farmers and tractors being swallowed by the earth when they went over an area where there was a peat fire beneath. I am not sure I believe it, but it is an interesting story.

At least one outfit on the Delta "farms" peat, digging it up from beneath the water off the San Joaquin. It is then barged to a site near Stockton, spread, dried then sacked to nourish the gardens of city folks.

Peat is very black and photographs beautifully to simulate explosions in movies. Many sacks of the stuff were shipped to Hawaii to be exploded in the movie Tora! Tora! Tora! Unfortunately, the hardworking guys who farm the Delta peat didn't get to go along.

The dictionary also defines peat as "A merry young girl; darling, used as an endearment." However, when I call my honey "Peatie" she doesn't think it's very funny, much less endearing.

5

Finding Your Way— Charts And Markers

Labyrinthine as the Delta may be, finding your way from hither to yon is no insurmountable task. To be sure, you may get temporarily lost now and again— it even happens to the old Delta pros. But most routes interconnect and you'll soon find yourself back on the right track again.

Consider my pal Reggie White. In his 34-foot Nautaline houseboat he was leading a group of eight or ten boats from Stockton on a run up the Mokelumne River's south fork for a raft-up at The Meadows. This is the shortest route and not very difficult.

Reggie was having a time, chatting with others in the flotilla over the marine radio. In fact, he was having so much fun that he soon found himself off-route on Beaver Slough. And every last member of the group (seasoned boaters all of 'em) followed Reggie down this pleasant dead-end slough. When the slough petered out, there was a minor traffic jam as all the boats tried to get turned around.

Reggie forgot to follow the "island navigation rule".

It goes like this. The Delta is populated with over half-a-hundred reclaimed islands. The entire perimeter of each is protected by a levee bank. Plot your course considering the island levee banks you must follow. And don't be lured by the smaller unleveed tule islands that can so easily get you lost.

For example, on Reggie's route you would turn right off the Stockton Deepwater Channel at light #11 (more on these later) onto Little Connection Slough. You will immediately pass the tiny Little Venice Island, coming next to Venice Island. Now you religeously keep this island's levee bank on your left.

At the obvious intersection of Potato Slough from the left, you continue straight

"switching" to the levee bank of Bouldin Island. Now keep this bank on your left to the intersection of the Mokelumne's south fork from the left just past the Highway 12 swing bridge.

Here again you "switch" to the levee bank of Staten Island, keeping it on your left till just past the bridge at Wimpy's. It was along this portion of the route that Reggie got careless. Sycamore, Hog and Beaver sloughs beckon. But by following the left bank, there is no way you can be shunted off into them.

This method will work for you going to most any place on the Delta. In a sudden winter fog, it will help get you back to port.

Charts And Maps

Most Delta houseboaters use the commercial maps for day-to-day cruising. They show placement of marinas and resorts, which are fine landmarks to confirm that you are on route. Schell Books produces and sells such a Delta Map and I am partial to it!

If you plan to do a lot of Delta cruising, it is also handy to have the official N.O.A.A. nautical charts sold at many marine supply stores. They contain a lot of detail, including water depths. Although resorts and marinas are not shown on the chart face.

Reading the maps and charts is not complicated. If you are not befuddled by the everyday road map, you'll have no difficulty.

Channel Markers

The Stockton Deepwater Channel, the Sacramento Ship Channel and the Sacramento River are marked by a system of consecutively numbered stationary markers that make it easy to

Markers such as the one above keep you on course in both the Sacramento and Stockton ship channels and the Sacramento River.

navigate these waters. The markers are commonly referred to as "lights" because most contain lights that blink on and off at night.

Proceeding "up river" from the ocean the red (even-numbered) markers are on your right and the green (odd-numbered) markers are on your left. They are indicated on maps and charts. They mark the deep water, and you won't go aground if you stay within their marked route. Just remember "red-right-returning".

Using Landmarks

Delta terrain is pool-table flat. High objects can be seen from afar and can help keep you on route. Mount Diablo is a towering sentinal off to the west. The television tower at Walnut Grove springs up into the ionosphere and serves as a landmark for anyone heading that way. Charts show the placement of the tall skinny power cable towers that feed electricity across key waterways. All can help you get your bearings—but also remember your compass!

Closer at hand are bridges, railroad crossings, highways, ferry crossings, public boat launching ramps, water towers, towns, marinas, parks and other things located on maps that can keep you from getting lost. Studying a map of the Delta is the next best thing to cruising its waters.

No-Wake And 5 mph Zones

A wake is the waves caused by your boat's motion while it is under way. It can cause considerable damage to boats tied to a dock or to one another. You are responsible for the damage it does. Ired recipients of wakes have been known to fire shotguns at offending boats.

Marina areas, ferry crossings and other places may be posted with 5 mph signs. Even if a dock area is not posted, you are required to slow to 5 mph if there is a boat docked to it and you are within 200 feet. Likewise with swimming areas. The sheriff and the Coast Guard can and will ticket violators.

If you have difficulty judging 5 mph, go very slowly and observe your wake. You don't want any of its action to reach the docks or berths. Be courteous.

Some Rules Of The Road

Keep to the right of boats approaching you. Boats to your right have the right of way. If necessary, slow down or stop to let them pass or cross in front of you.

Cruise to the right of an imaginary line down the center of the waterway, while not getting too close to the shoreline.

Keep oncoming boats to your left, passing "port-to-port".

When overtaking another boat, sound one horn blast if passing on the right and two if on the left.

Be especially watchful of water skiers. If one falls in front of you, swing to miss him and immediately shift to neutral. Slow down if a ski boat is displaying a red flag or a member is holding an arm in the air. This means a skier or tow rope is in the water.

6

Planning Your Cruise Itinerary

You are ready now to start your exploration of the Delta. You've pored over maps and charts. You know about channel markers and levee-bank navigation. Your boat's fuel is topped off and the cooler is brimful of ice.

All you need is a cruise plan. I like to pick destinations that are not much over a three-hour cruise away. That would be about 25 miles at 10 mph, allowing for slow zones along the way. Plug into this time spent on an off-course excursion or two, a stop for a picnic and swim, a marina stop for last-minute supplies, and you see that a good portion of a day can lazily, enjoyably be eaten up.

It is a good idea to plan your cruises for two days in advance so that you won't have to do a lot of doubling back over the same water. This lets you see more and experience more during the same period of time.

If you can plan a marina stop on each route, so much the better. This will let you top off your fuel and water and buy ice and other supplies. Bridges along your route are a key factor. Consult our chart and see that any in your path will either open or clear your boat. If clearance is marginal on a bridge not openable, then you may have to plan to arrive there at or near low tide for maximum clearance.

Even if you are an old salt of a Delta boater, it is fun to try different routes to your favorite destinations. So what if they are a bit longer. You will find new and interesting territory along the way.

But don't be a slave to your cruise plan. If you find a pleasant spot along the way where you'd like to stay for a day or so—do it! Lazy exploration is part of what boating the Delta is all about. You should feel unfettered. Able to change plans on a whim.

Water Depth Worriers

If you haven't churned mud, dinged a prop, been lost, got stuck on a sand bar or been left high and dry by an outgoing tide in the Delta, then you have not yet earned the right to call yourself a river rat.

Nothing ventured, not much gained. There is at least a tiny element of risk involved the instant you leave familiar waters. If you only "go where you know", you'll never get to see new places.

Concern over adequate water depth keeps too many boaters plying the same old water every weekend. Too bad. Let's look at some of the factors to be considered.

First you should know how much water depth your boat requires. That is, how much it "draws". On a rental boat, be sure to ask about this. Most houseboats fortunately draw considerably less than cruisers of comparable size.

We know that the deep water shipping channels have over 25-foot depths within their marked channels. And that mean lowtide water depths are marked on the official N.O.A.A. charts (not however, on the extreme south Delta portion of the chart).

We know that water depth can be three to five feet deeper at high tide. Thus in some waters you might cruise with more care at low tide and with more abandon at high tide.

If your boat has a depth finder, keep an eye on it when in unfamiliar waters. When the water starts to shallow, slow down to an idle and "feel" your way along. If you think you're going aground, shift into neutral to protect the prop. In shallow water with no depth finder, you can use a boat pole off the bow to prod the bottom and measure depth.

Wherever there is a levee, you can

assume that it was built up by a clamshell dredge digging up bottom mud. So the water ought to have good depth about 20 feet out from the levee.

Don't short cut across strings of tule islands punctuated by short stretches of water. Cut a wide path on the outside of bends in the rivers to miss possible shoals.

Practically speaking, there are good deep routes to places all over the Delta. They are regularly plied by deep-draft vessels and even sail boats with formidable keels. With a modicum of caution, a boater can get most anywhere. The whole Delta ought to be considered your playground.

Several No Nos

Most rental houseboats are not allowed below the Antioch bridge as a condition of their insurance policies. Below the bridge, the river broadens and can become rough on windy days. This is a favored fishing area, especially by fishermen in quest of the mighty sturgeon. There are only a handful of places in this area that houseboat owners are wont to visit. It is considered pretty much on the fringe of Delta houseboating territory. Most Delta owner-houseboat policies limit vessels to above the Carquinez bridge without special permission.

Franks Tract, adjacent to Bethel island, is off limits to most rental houseboats. Owners can safely traverse the Tract if they know where to enter and depart it without grinding props on the old submerged levees. But this is no place to be on a windy day—even the river route mailman foresakes it then! White caps of mighty proportions can quickly appear.

The Cross Delta Channel (called the Locke Canal by some) adjacent to the Walnut Grove towering T.V. antenna, is also off limits to rental houseboats. This channel, between Snodgrass Slough and the Sacramento, was dug for flood control. It has a pair of gates that are at times closed to regulate water flow. Even when open, clearance at the gates will not normally be adequate to accommodate many houseboats. Current moves fast here.

However, this is an ideal short cut from The Meadows area into the Sacramento River system for anyone with a low-bridge boat. I use it all the time with my runabout, especially for access to the upper end of Georgiana Slough.

Favorite Cruises

A minor problem in mapping out cruises for publication is that not all boaters will be starting from the same place. I tend to think in terms of starting down river a few miles from Stockton because that is near to where I live and keep my boats.

These cruises aren't necessarily meant to be duplicated (although they can be) but to serve as guides. They may be altered to suit your own particular tastes and circumstances.

The Meadows Cruise

Duration: 2½ to 3 hours. No question about it, The Meadows is the best known anchorage area in the Delta. The late Erle Stanley Gardner sang its praises both orally and in print when he was roaming the Delta in his flotilla of River Queen houseboats. Its popularity has perservered. And it is covered in detail in the Outstanding Anchorages chapter.

From the San Joaquin, you have a choice of two routes to The Meadows, the Mokelumne River's North and South forks. The South Fork is the shorter and I most often go by it and return by the North Fork to vary the route. Both are pleasant, deep water, meandering waterways with plenty of low-tide beaches that beckon you to stop for a swim and a picnic.

You depart from the San Joaquin River (also called the Stockton Deepwater Channel) at Light #11 onto Little Connection Slough. Just past the Venice island cable-drawn ferry is Herman & Helen's, a full-service marina with groceries and a cafe.

You continue onto Little Potato Slough and eventually to the ghost town of Terminous. Here is Tower Park Marina, a sprawling complex with a restaurant, cocktail lounge, grocery store and anything else you might require. I always consider this about mid-point on the cruise.

At one time Terminous was a key railway produce shipping center where

L. Tower Park is a good stop on the way to The Meadows. Below. The good life in The Meadows.

about 4,000 workers and their families lived in a box car city. As many as 10,000 workers labored there on some days, shipping some 20,000 carloads of produce in a year. When trucking replaced the railroad, it pulled up its tracks and the town died.

The Highway 12 swing bridge is just above Tower Park. At non-opening hours and seasons, you may have to catch the tide right to clear it (see bridge chart). You pick up the Moke's South Fork just above the bridge and can see the ramps from another cable ferry that was discontinued a few years ago. Less than a mile from here is an appendage off your right that makes a fine overnight anchorage locally referred to as "the bedroom". A while back it was dredged to be developed as a county-run fishing and anchorage area now called Westgate Landing.

Miles later you'll encounter a bridge just before Wimpy's. It doesn't open, but clearance is good. Wimpy's has a good restaurant and a busy cocktail lounge. The fuel dock is roomy and there is usually docking help. But pay heed to the strong current that moves through here.

If you stay to the right, you'll be going up the Mokelumne (this is where the river forks) and immediately pass New Hope Landing with its fuel dock and mini-Super Market.

But to continue toward The Meadows, you should have stayed to the left bank here and then taken the next right a short distance farther. This will take you around tiny Dead Horse Island and feed you onto Snodgrass Slough just below the Cross Delta. You'll follow the right bank here into the area Gardner called "The California Everglades".

One of frail heart can lose courage

here. The waterway narrows. The brush hangs close and fallen trees poke up out of the water. You expect to see crocodiles slithering into the water. But water depths are good. Soon the slough widens and a mammoth railroad bridge looms into sight. This bridge remains open these days and is slated for eventual removal. To its right is Lost Slough, a fine remote anchorage that offers no land access.

You continue under (through) the bridge, staying to the left into yet more Everglades. Shortly it opens up and you see land dead ahead. You have arrived at The Meadows Slough, which stretches almost straight arrow off to your left.

Cruise To The Riverboat

Duration: approximately two hours. All routes eventually lead to John Moore's Riverboat, a renovated 156-foot freighter that serves as a floating restaurant on the lower Mokelumne. It's a good place to dine and dance and overnight at the docks out front.

Returning from The Meadows, you back track until you reach the Cross Delta, and after that you follow the right bank. You'll pass Walnut Grove Marina with its Snack Barge, easy access fuel dock and well-stocked grocery store.

Cap'n John's Riverboat.

Next is Giusti's, a fine Italian restaurant and bar that was Gardner's favorite hangout. The current is strong here and be sure to move in against it when docking.

Just after Giusti's you leave Snodgrass for the Moke's North Fork, passing under a swing bridge (consult bridge chart). From here you leave civilization behind, for there are no more water establishments for a long while. The river is broad, sees plenty of traffic and there are few opportunities to get off route.

Eventually the South Fork joins and the river becomes one again. Shortly thereafter, meandering Georgiana Slough feeds in from your right. You pass bustling B & W Resort with its cafe, fuel dock and cabins, almost in the shadow of the Highway 12 bridge. Then in quick succession are Perry's, Rancho Marina, Lighthouse Resort (cafe, RV Park, fuel dock), Willow Berm Marina (spacious and easy fuel dock) and then the Riverboat. Next is Korth's Pirates Lair, a beautiful marina with fuel and cafe, but tight to get into for novice boaters.

At one time there was a thriving village of Chinese inhabitants called Central City located across the water from Moore's. But it went under during floods of the thirties and the city's remaining buildings were hauled off.

Sometimes I reverse this Meadows run and stop at Moore's for breakfast in the morning on the way. You will re-enter the San Joaquin near Light #53. If you head down river (watch out for the shoals) you quickly encounter Happy Harbor, Andreas Cove Marina (good overnight stops), Spindrift Marina (fine food, tight docking) and Blue Heron Harbor, all in a couple miles. Eddo's Harbor at Gallager Slough is next.

Cruise To
Walnut Grove & Ryde

Duration: 1½ to 2 hours. From the Riverboat, or even Bethel Island and up the San Joaquin toward Stockton, you are positioned nicely to take one of my favorites, Georgiana Slough, to Walnut Grove and beyond.

I once looked down upon this slough from high atop the Walnut Grove T.V. antenna and marvelled at how closely it parallels the meanderings of the neighboring Sacramento River.

Jack London used to spend summers writing aboard a houseboat on Georgiana. Paddlewheelers making the run between Sacramento and Stockton used it because it was the shortest route—well, almost the shortest. During flood time they would cut across some of the islands using "wheatfield navigation"!

There is a feeling of remoteness to Georgiana. Until recently, it harbored not a single commercial establishment. But now, after 15 years in the planning stages, you'll find Ox Bow Marina, a deluxe marina and waterside mobile home park built into the slough's natural oxbow. It has covered berthing, fuel, a yacht brokerage and other facilities. In the future, it will have a motel and restaurant.

There are three bridges on Georgiana, one of which is a single leaf bascule-type railroad bridge that has always remained in the open position, except when trains

A petite rental boat slips under the Walnut Grove drawbridge.

L. The active Ryde Hotel. Below. A trawler makes its way up the Sacramento out of Walnut Grove.

pass. It is on the same recently abandoned line as The Meadows bridge and has just been torn down.

The Walnut Grove merchants have an excellent guest dock on the Sacramento's east bank. You can overnight there or park to shop and explore the town. The Chinese hamlet of Locke is about a mile trek up the levee road. Tony's restaurant is just across the street from the dock.

Less than three miles down the Sacramento river is the sleepy hamlet of Ryde. At one time Ryde was a thriving little community, regularly visited by paddlewheelers. It had its own asparagus cannery. Now, about the only activity there is at the historic 50-room Ryde

hotel. You can tie at its dock out front, have a libation at the bar, or dine in its restaurant.

Cruise To
Steamboat Slough

Duration: One to two hours, depending on where you stop. Ah, there is the magic of nostalgia in its name. And you can see still the paddlewheelers thrashing up the 12-mile slough that served as a short cut for the steamboats on the Sacramento run, handily chopping off a full six miles from the river route.

Out of Walnut Grove you head up the Sacramento for about six miles to the huge double-leaf bascule drawbridge that

The action's at the Steamboat bridge.

guards the slough's entrance. Above the bridge is Steamboat Landing, a comfortable place with cocktails, food, fuel and amiable company. The sandy beach at the bridge is a part of this fine operation and there's guest docking. Below the bridge on the opposite bank, is Steamboaters with its long dock and imposing building up on the levee. It has fallen on hard times and at this writing has been closed for most of a season with no plans now for reopening.

Across the slough is a long string of boats at anchor, nuzzled into the brushy shore. The upper section of Steamboat Slough is an active place on summer weekends.

A pleasant aside from here, is a short run up to the comfortable little village of Courtland, fronting on the Sacramento River. You can park at the Courtland Docks, where there's a good restaurant, and browse around the few shops in town.

Current is swift both here and on Steamboat. So figure it right when docking. Farther down Steamboat, past Sutter Slough, is Snuggle Inn, with food and fuel. A few miles farther is Hidden Harbor with food and fuel. That antebellum edifice you passed early on the slough is River Mansion and is no longer open to the public.

Cruise To
Rio Vista Via Miner Slough

Duration: Three to four hours. Most boaters would continue down Steamboat for an almost straight run to Rio Vista, then proceed across Threemile Slough to the San Joaquin at Light No. 34, down river a few miles from where we first started The Meadows cruise. This string of cruises would cover a lot of Delta with almost no backtracking.

But I and some of my river rat pals have become fond of detouring via Miner Slough to visit Islands Marina, a quiet place to lunch, sip concoctions made from wine, and maybe even overnight.

You head down Steamboat from River Mansion, taking the first right to double back on what is Sutter Slough. At the next "intersection" you stay to the left onto Miner Slough on which there is a bridge to reckon with. In short time you will reach the Islands. You'll spot a low bridge dead ahead, but don't fret over it. Signs on it will point you around one of the islands and into the spacious guest dock.

Continuing down Miner about four miles, if you watch carefully off to your right, you'll spot the towering A-frame from an old dredge, seemingly rotting back in the underbrush. This is the *Golden Gate,* a great old dredge that has been magnificently converted into a first-class facility with beer, wine, soft drinks and sandwiches. A fine overnight stop with plenty of room for wandering ashore. Good water depths.

Continue on Miner, which will feed you into Cache Slough and the channel for Sacramento-bound freighters. You'll pass

Author rides a water buffalo as Grand Marshal (not the buffalo) of the Rio Vista Bass Derby Parade.

48

Golden Gate Island Resort on Miner Slough is one of those stops you will want to make.

the *Real McCoy*, a diesel ferry that is free running rather than on cable, and then go on into the Sacramento. Don't be misled by the river's breadth here. There are sandbars lurking inches below the surface to catch boaters who stray from the marked deep-water channel.

You'll pass under the great lift bridge at Rio Vista. This is one fine little town with comfortable little shops and stately old homes. Unfortunately, the town itself has only a modest guest dock and is not really suited for overnighting. You can stop off nearby at the guest docks of Delta Marina behind The Point Restaurant and stroll into town if you wish (ask about the shortcut). This makes a good overnight.

Your cross over to the San Joaquin at Threemile Slough is down river about three miles. The Outrigger Marina on Threemile is an excellent overnight stop. It has fuel and other supplies. Its restaurant serves good food and you can partake of cocktails at its active saloon. Tables at its super deck are popular in the summer. Current is swift here.

The Scheme Of All These Cruises

Okay, if you carefully study my cruise offerings thus far, you'll see that many can be handled in bits and dabs over long weekends. Or all of them could be strung out for most of a week's vacation. You could delete portions. Or even combine two cruises into a single, longer day.

There are some important areas yet to cover, including my favorite haunts off the San Joaquin near Stockton, busy Bethel Island and the more remote south Delta. You can combine all or some of these with all or some of the cruises already mentioned.

The central San Joaquin River sees a lot of traffic on summer weekends because waterways to many places in the Delta feed into it. I try to avoid long runs on it when possible, because on weekends you will spend a lot of time wrestling with wakes from other boats.

Cruise The Back Way To Bethel

Duration: Two hours or less. Stockton area boaters bound for Bethel Island traditionally head down the San Joaquin, then cross over on Old River along the near edge of Franks Tract. I have a better, faster, less trafficked, more scenic route. Ah, but the many times I got lost back there among the tules on this route. That was before I learned about levee-bank navigation. Now I only occasionally get lost there!

We start at Light No. 24 on the San Joaquin and slip around the back side of 52-acre Lost Isle to head southwest on Turner Cut, religiously keeping McDonald Island's levee bank on our right. We pass Turner Cut Resort (good food and fuel) a cable-drawn ferry, then Tiki Lagun (cocktails, food). These are the last two fuel stops before Bethel.

You continue, taking a right onto the very straight Empire Cut. To the left is

49

You slip around the back side of 52-acre Lost Isle.

Whiskey Slough, a pleasant little dead-end slough with a nice marina at its end. McDonald Island is home for one of the largest gas reservoirs in North America. In May of 1974 a well blew and burned for 18 days before fire fighter Red Adair was imported from Texas by P.G. & E. to snuff it out. You can see four giant cylindrical tanks poking skyward like missile silos.

The game plan is to keep McDonald's (also called Henning Tract) levee on your right. Leave Empire by turning right first chance onto Latham Slough (where in an earlier chapter, friend Alex lost his anchor) following the right bank for a couple miles until a huge old black barge-like cable-drawn ferry looms dead ahead. This privately owned behemoth shuffles farm equipment and crop-ladened semi-trucks between McDonald and Mandeville islands.

Turn to the left in front of this ferry and begin to keep the levee bank of 5440-acre Mandeville Island on your right. You are now on Connection Slough (not to be confused with Little Connection way over by Herman & Helen's) and you will soon encounter the only privately owned and operated swing bridge on the Delta. It is

manned round the clock all year (sometimes casually, however).

Here and there along the levee you have seen weathered old farm buildings, most of them still in use. The imposing multi-story rectangular barracks building you pass is Camp 27.

Just short of Franks Tract, a 3177-acre island that went under with the winter floods of 1937-38 and has stayed under since, there used to be the body of a yellow "bracero" bus imbedded in the levee to ward off what was once an impending break.

If you are headed for "down town" Bethel Island, you turn left just short of the Tract and follow the remains of the levee on Old River, then Sand Mound Slough (be careful here not to get shunted onto the long straight Holland Cut), then Dutch Slough and finally the bridge linking Bethel to the outside world.

Of course, Bethel Island boat owners and skippers of rental boats, can reverse this route for the quickest access to the bustling Stockton area, with maybe a planned destination of Lost Isle, Windmill Cove or some of the fine anchorages in that area.

Cruising To
The South Delta

Duration: up to five hours, one way. No portion of the Delta's 1,000 miles of waterways is less known and more neglected by houseboaters than the south Delta. Commercial maps of the area are oft times poorly detailed. Even the official N.O.A.A. chart of the area (no. 18661) only carries an inset of part of the area and with no water depths marked.

Yet I have several river joints I like to visit down that way. All would suffice for an overnight. Water depths are fine for houseboats and cruisers using care. The bridges can be dealt with.

Stop number one is Middle River Inn, a decrepit place by some boaters' standards. But I love it and many good times have been had there. To get there, proceed as in the "Bethel" cruise, but do not leave Empire at Latham Slough. Instead, cruise on past the private cable ferry and now keep to the left bank. Almost imperceptibly you will enter the waters of Middle River.

Keeping to the left bank you'll pass the Bacon Island swing bridge, then Bullfrog Landing (fuel, beer & wine). Next an ominous looking railroad bridge will cut off your route. Clearance is often too little for houseboats and the bridge isn't manned. If you can't clear, turn right just in front of the bridge and follow the tracks for about a mile to the Old River railroad bridge which is manned on two shifts or left partially opened.

Pass through, turn left and retrace that mile run now on the opposite side of the railroad to Middle River Inn. Warning, tie only out near the end of the dock to be sure of adequate water depth.

From here you can follow the left bank all the way to Union Point (famous for its shark feed, at the Hwy. 4 bridge. It has food & cocktails. You'll have passed another cable ferry. And if you nose into one of the coves to the right, you are apt to see Berkeley Water Ski Club members jumping off a ramp they maintain in the area.

Leave Union Point with enough fuel, for stops are few in this area. You may have to catch the tide right to clear this unopenable bridge. Slide under it, staying slightly to the right for the long straight run on Victoria Canal. Continue past Coney Island and its small neighboring island, turning left to run along the edge of Clifton Court Forebay. We are heading to Oasis Marina. And if you short cut around some to these islands, you are apt to encounter mud bars.

You'll pass the pumping station where Delta water is pumped out to provide

R. "Dragon Lady" joins the festivities for opening of the new Discovery Bay Yacht Harbor, eventually to have over 600 berths. R. above. Tracy Oasis Marina's annual Delta Dip February waterski run.

irrigation and drinking water for communities far away. Dead ahead is Del's Harbor, a busy place crowded with water skiers during the summer. Turn left onto Grant Line Canal (there's a white house on the point). Oasis is about halfway up the Canal and has everything you might need.

You can return via Fabian & Bell Canal and then over the same route past Coney Island. Now continue onto Old River through the Highway 4 bridge (opens on at least one shift all year). An interesting aside here is to take a left on Indian Slough to have a look at Discovery Bay, a splendid development of waterfront homes with private boat docks. Its new Discovery Bay Yacht Harbor is a full-service marina with fuel, a restaurant, marine supplies and much more. It can make an excellent overnight stop.

To the right off Indian is Orwood Resort, in the summer crowded with ski boats. A careful houseboater can get down there, but don't turn into the harbor toward the fuel docks.

Old River will soon deliver you back to the railroad Bridge a mile from Middle River Inn. From here you could feed back into the original route to the San Joaquin. It's a handy run from here to Bethel Island too, via Holland Cut. It should be clear that Bethel boats could easily have joined our south Delta cruise at this point, also.

Because of the many tule islands in this area, it is important to use levee-bank navigation to keep from getting lost. Remember though, those same tule islands offer endless fine overnight anchorages.

"Disco Bay's" boat stacker.

Discovery Bay Yacht Harbor Now Leasing

"The Delta's Prestige Marina"

The Delta's newest & most modern marina is now accepting reservations for the new phase of deep water berths. Group berthing available, so get your friends together.

- 112 berths to 50 feet; covered $4/berth ft., uncovered $3/berth ft. (650 berths when completed)
- Each with water, storage & 30 amp elec. (metered)
- Two-lane launching
- Roomy guest dock
- Fuel dock: diesel-regular-premium
- Restaurant, marine supplies, gifts, yacht & boat sales

"Most Modern Dry Stack Storage Facility On The Delta"

- Accommodates 150 boats to 23 feet (390 units when completed)
- Convenient forklift launching
- Safe & easy on boats
- Only $30 a month
- Call ahead and your boat can be gassed and in the water waiting for you

On Hwy 4 between Antioch and Stockton. For more information, call (415)

634-5928

Margo's   OVERLOOKING THE WATER   OPEN 7 DAYS
                                            ALL YEAR

Harbor Galley

at the all-new
Discovery Bay Yacht Harbor
Excellent Cuisine In An Informal Atmosphere
Lunch & Dinner Daily - Breakfast Weekends
Sunday Brunch - Daily Specials
Take-Out Deli
Let Us Cater Your Next Special Affair

GUEST
DOCKING   **(415) 634-1358**   CAR
                                                      PARKING

7

Bridges Of The Delta

Sprinkled around the Delta and its tributaries are maybe 70 bridges. They lend character to the Delta. Now and then one can block your cruising route. Most of the bridges open. But some don't. Those that open are called drawbridges.

We cultivate three types of drawbridges here. First there's the ubiquitous swing bridge that looks frail and almost homemade. These open by swinging sideways like an old railroad turntable. In the process they groan and tremble, but they do their job in a workmanlike way. The longest swing bridge in existence spans the Mississippi, a railroad bridge opening 525 feet.

My favorite Delta swing bridge resides on Connection Slough. This decrepit old structure is privately owned and operated. Years ago it was retired from service on the Grant Line Canal, purchased for the rumored sum of one buck, then dismantled and moved here to replace a pontoon bridge that nobody much cared for. The bridgetender will trudge out to open it for you round the clock all year long. Wave to him when you pass through.

Bascule bridges are more impressive. They open like the ancient drawbridges over castle moats. They feature massive concrete counterweights that make opening power requirements little or nothing. The French word "bascule" means a child's seesaw, and that pretty much explains how these bridges work. The Tower of London bridge is perhaps the best known of this style. There are single-leaf bascules with one opening span and double leaves with two.

The third type, the vertical lift drawbridge, is more scarce on the Delta. It can be recognized by its pair of high towers that house counterweights equal to the exact weight of the lift span. They are efficient and fast, only needing to open high enough to let a vessel pass under.

The lift bridge at Rio Vista will rise 138 feet above the water and has as many as 3,000 openings in a year. Fog-bound freighters occasionally crash into Delta bridges.

When a few years ago this happened to the old Antioch Bridge (yes, this is the one most rental houseboaters can't go beyond), the tender was trapped high up in his cubicle for 18 hours. When he got back to *terra firma*, he took up another line of work.

Some bridges are not tended, and others are only at certain hours and times of the year. Although there is often an alternate route to where you want to go, you need to consider these bridges when planning your cruises. Otherwise you are apt to find your passage blocked by an untended bridge offering 10 feet clearance while your boat requires 13 feet!

It is a good idea to know the height of your boat above the water line. Measure it closely, then permanently post it at a visible spot on the helm. It'll be posted here on many rental houseboats too.

Passing under a bridge with only a couple inches of clearance to spare can be risky business. The wake from a passing boat can send the top of your boat banging into the bridge and do considerable damage. It is a good idea to clear the upper deck of any passengers. Too, deck-chair manufacturers do a tidy business replacing chairs that skippers forgot were on the upper deck till a chair-eating bridge plunked them into the water! Many a cooler has met the same sad fate too.

L. A trawler tweaks under the Walnut Grove bascule bridge. Below. A bridge "meter rod" shows clearance in feet.

Getting 'Em To Open

Fortunately, most of the key draw-bridges are manned (or womanned) much of the daylight hours at least during the prime boating season. If clearance is inadequate or marginal, all you have to do is give one prolonged blast of the horn (about four seconds) followed by a short blast of about a second. The bridge tender will reply with the same signal, or with five or more short blasts as the danger signal. Given the open signal, you should hang well back and wait for the bridge to open. Given no signal at all, wait a few minutes, then toot the open signal again.

Bridges marked with an asterisk on our chart also respond to radio calls on chan-nel nine (they may also monitor channel 16, but nine is their talk channel). Using the radio, no horn signal is required. But you must continue to monitor channel nine until you have passed through and are on your way.

You will find it one great thrill and feeling of power to see a giant bridge swing or yawn open for you. I can never get enough of it.

Bridge Clearance

The meter rod is a flat board with clearance in feet painted on it and it is posted at most bridges. Where the water level is on it gives you clearance at that particular time. And naturally, this changes with the tide.

Some Delta maps and charts indicate the high-water and low-water clearances

of bridges. It may be marked 4'/17' or H.W. 4 ft., L.W. 17 ft. for example. My observations are that these readings are most often unrealistic.

So we have compiled a table of more realistic readings. Use them with judge-ment. They are not the bible. They will be inaccurate for plus tides and during times of flood or heavy spring runoff. The table also shows opening times and hours for the bridges and any special opening instructions.

When charting your cruise where there will be untended bridges, estimate what the tide position will be when you arrive—Delta tide tables are helpful for this. Check our table to find the usual *high-tide* clearance of the bridges. If you are still in doubt about being able to clear an

55

untended bridge, telephone a nearby marina before making a long cruise. Or chart an alternate route.

Should you care to know more about the intricacies of Delta bridges, write for the Coast Guard's free booklet, *Bridge Regulations in Northern California* to: Twelfth Coast Guard District, 630 Sansome St., San Francisco, CA 94126.

A high-clearance rental houseboat "toots open" the Little Potato Slough swing bridge.

High Water Bridge Clearances - Delta

Bridge Location	When Tended	Hours	Usual High Tide Clearance
Little Potato Sl. at Tower Park	5-1 thru 10-31	6 a.m.-10 p.m.	11 ft.
S. Fork of Mokelumne at Wimpy's	Normally Unopenable		13 ft.
N. Fork of Mokelumne at Giusti's	5-1 thru 10-31	9 a.m. - 5 p.m.	11½ ft.
Private on N. Fork of Mokelumne	Normally Unopenable		9½ ft.
Snodgrass Sl.-Twin Cities Rd.	Normally Unopenable		17 ft.
Delta Cross Channel Note: Gates Sometimes Closed	Unopenable		8½ ft.
Steamboat Slough	5-1 thru 10-31	6 a.m.-10 p.m.	18 ft.
Sutter Slough	Normally Unopenable		19 ft.
Miner Slough	12 hr. notice		17 ft.
Sacramento Riv. RR at Sacto.	5-1 thru 10-31 11-1 thru 4-30	6 a.m.-10 p.m.	28 ft.
*Sacramento Riv. Tower Br.	Same as above	Same as above	34 ft.
*Sacramento Riv. at Freeport	Same as above	Same as above	34 ft.
*Sacramento Riv. at Paintersville	Same as above	Same as above	18 ft.
*Sacramento Riv. at Walnut Grove	Same as above	Same as above	16 ft.
*Sacramento Riv. at Isleton	Same as above	Same as above	16 ft.
*Sacramento Riv. at Rio Vista	24 hours		19½ ft.
*Threemile Slough	24 hours		13 ft.
Georgiana Sl. at Sacramento Riv.	5-1 thru 10-31 11-1 thru 4-30	6 a.m.-10 p.m. 9 a.m.- 5 p.m.	14 ft.
Georgiana Sl. near Isleton	5-1 thru 10-31 11-1 thru 4-30	6 a.m.-10 p.m. 9 a.m.-5 p.m.	9 ft.
*Mokelumne Riv. at Hwy. 12	5-1 thru 10-31 11-1 thru 4-30	6 a.m.-10 p.m. 9 a.m.-5 p.m.	12 ft.
Bethel Island Bridge	Normally Unopenable		16½ ft.
Connection Slough Bridge	24 hours		6 ft.
Middle River-Bacon Island	5-15 thru 9-15 (Every Day) 9-16 thru 5-14 Thurs. thru Mon.	9 a.m.-5 p.m. 9 a.m.-5 p.m.	10 ft.
Middle River RR Bridge	12 hour notice		10½ ft.
Middle River at Hwy. 4	Normally Unopenable		12 ft.
Old River Bridge RR Bridge	24 hours		16½ ft.
Old River at Hwy. 4	5-1 thru 10-31 11-1 thru 4-30	6 a.m.-10 p.m. 9 a.m.-5 p.m.	11½ ft.
14 Mile Sl. at Paradise Point	Normally Unopenable		20½ ft.
Bishop Cut at 8 Mile Rd.	12 hour notice		5½ ft.
Honker Cut at King Island	12 hour notice		8 ft.

8

Dining On The Delta

Some time ago I did a magazine article titled *A Gourmet's Guide To Dining On The Delta*. When Hal Proctor, a boating friend, read the piece he commented to his first mate that I was infinitely better equipped to do a guide to eating hamburgers on the Delta.

Well, I have nothing against hamburgers, and I confess that, although I like to dine as regally as I can afford to, the tag gourmet doesn't fit comfortably. Hal Proctor would most likely have been pleased with the article title as I originally submitted it. In it, I used *gourmand's guide* instead of *gourmet's guide!*

In any case, some very good dining awaits you on the Delta. The first mate will appreciate the time off from galley duty. And best of all, you can often boat right up to the restaurant door step. A casual air prevails. And whatever you are wearing, as long as it includes shirt and shoes, will usually be acceptable attire.

At times, the casualness appears to extend to the hours of business. Some places are closed one or more days per week. Several have seasonal liquor licenses which require that they close or not sell liquor at least three months out of the year. Winter open days and hours are often curtailed. So to avoid being disappointed, phone ahead before making a long run specifically to dine.

Al's Place, (916) 776-1800, in the Chinese hamlet of Locke on the Sacramento River, everywhere is known irreverently as, Al-The-Wop's. Fare here is uncomplicated, as is everything else about the place. You enter through a saloon, with its high ceiling festooned with thumb-tacked dollar bills. It'll cost you a buck to find out how the bartender gets 'em up on that 20-foot ceiling. A

The deck at P.J.'s at Courtland Docks.

dusty stuffed ostrich stares down at you from its perch.

Somehow the food is always good at Al's. Lunches are served daily, 11:30 to 2 p.m., steak sandwiches only. Tables are set with jars of peanut butter and marmalade, and after awhile you become addicted to the stuff spread on Al's hot French bread. The dinner menu contains only steak and it is served with all the trimmings and it is big. Dinner service is 5 to 10 p.m. weekdays, 5 to 11 p.m. Fridays and Saturdays and 3 to 10 p.m. Sundays. Closed Easter, Thanksgiving, and Christmas eve and day. For a per-foot fee, you can tie your boat to the guest dock at the Boathouse in Locke or make the trek of about a mile from Walnut Grove merchants dock.

The Anchor, (415) 684-2404, on Piper Slough at Bethel Island, behind the levee at Frank's Marina. Breakfasts starts at 10 a.m. weekdays, 8 a.m. weekends and include omelettes and even homemade biscuits and gravy. Luncheon fare includes a variety of sandwiches and the popular half-pound Anchor Burger. Dinners are 5 to 10 p.m., 11 p.m. weekends in summer and till 9 p.m. winter weekdays. You can get fresh prawns done in beer batter, teriyaki chicken, New York steaks and red snapper. There's clam chowder every Friday and minestrone daily. Guest docking w/electricity at Frank's Marina.

Andreas Cove, (916) 777-6409, is located on the San Joaquin River next to Spindrift, just down from the Mokelumne. A comfortable family-type atmosphere prevails here and there is a downstairs (out of ear-shot) game arcade for the kids. Breakfast fare is hearty and three-egg omelettes are featured. Lunches include hot and cold sandwiches, soups and salads.

There is a special of the evening that changes from day to day on the dinner menu and is posted monthly on a calendar. Included are such as BBQ spare ribs, sirloin tips, roast beef, Swiss steak, et cetera. You can also order spaghetti, steaks, or sandwiches. Char-broiled steaks are a specialty. Weather permitting, you can dine outside on the new deck overlooking the river. Beer and wine only. Children's plates, closed Wednesdays. Guest docking, with electricity.

Artist Table, (415) 684-3414, at Viking Harbor on Dutch Slough near Bethel island, is a tiny restaurant tucked behind the levee. No more than forty diners can be seated and the atmosphere is intimate, the service congenial. You are pampered and the food is truly gourmet fare.

You can feast on pork chops stuffed with a special herb stuffing, Chateaubriand for two, scampi, trout almondine, scallops, lobster, rack of lamb and much more. The pace is leisurely with champagne vernique after the soup and salad, then a dessert wine after dinner. Desserts may vary from chocolate truffles to German cakes. The place has no liquor

license, but you'd never know it by the drinks—Margaritas, mai tais, etc. (Ask about the Dutch-Slough-Blue For Two).

Dinners are served year around. Wednesdays through Sundays, beginning at 5:30. Closing hours vary with the crowd, but the final seating is usually around 9 to 10 p.m. Reservations recommended. Limited guest docking and it is best to call to make arrangements.

A. J. Bump's Freeport Saloon, (916) 665-2251, in the Sacramento River town of Freeport, was established in 1863. You dock at Freeport Marina (by special arrangement, if there's room) for a trek of some 700 yards. There is both a saloon and a restaurant in a venerable old two-story building. The walls are covered with early-day Delta photos. The dress is casual.

Food is excellent and reasonably priced. The menu is varied and there is both luncheon and dinner service daily. Entrees are named after former owners of the saloon or early residents of the town, such as "Kirtlan's Beef Burgundy" after Tom Kirtlan, former town blacksmith.

Chez Zabeth is situated in the new Grocers Warehouse building at Waterfront Yacht Harbor at the Channel head in Stockton, scheduled for a July 1982 opening. It is a classic French cafe with authentic French country-style food. Zabeth does all the cooking and lends a touch of European charm from her homeland.

The menu is varied and includes a wide assortment of crepe dishes and specials of the day. Beer and wines. Breakfast and lunch are served Tuesday thru Sunday. Special "soirees" (dinner parties) are open to the public and are held on weekend evenings. Guest docking w/electricity.

Courtyard, (415) 684-2131, next to Bethel Island just west of the bridge, serves food with a flair in its Green House

Most anything you are wearing, as long as it includes shoes and shirts, will suffice at most Delta restaurants. These folks are all dolled up for the annual Classic Yacht Assn. Delta Rendezvous.

restaurant. You can dine inside in either of two tastefully decorated rooms or outside under umbrellas at cable-spool tables. Brunch is served Saturdays and Sundays 10 to 3:00 p.m. and includes fare such as eggs Benedict or egg souffle.

Lunches include a variety of fine sandwiches, salads and special dishes. Dinners are served Friday, Saturday and Sunday only one sitting, a maximum of 18 persons served, call for reservations. The menu is graced by such dishes as lapin aux amandes (rabbit cooked French style) and beef Wellington for two. Beer and wine. There's an ice cream parlor and a downstairs gift shop and art gallery. There is a designated guest berth at Richard's Yacht Center next door and it is okay to dock at the gas dock after it is closed.

Ernies, (916) 777-6510, is located "downtown" in the sleepy Sacramento River hamlet of Isleton. And this comfortable saloon and restaurant is favored by many Deltaphiles. The dinner menu is uncomplicated with but a choice of sirloin steak or broasted chicken (or try to coax the chef into thawing out one of the place's delicious homemade pasties, a meat-pie of a meal). Luncheon, served weekdays only from 11:30 a.m. to 1:30 p.m., offers a different special each day, plus a variety of hot sandwiches varying from French dip to hamburgers.

Dinner service is 5 to 9 p.m. weekdays, but to 10 p.m. Fridays and Sundays and 11 p.m. Saturdays. Overnight guest dock with electricity and from there it is 317 steps to Ernie's—or so the sign says.

The Fish Market is situated in the new Grocers Warehouse building at Waterfront Yacht Harbor at the Channel head in Stockton, scheduled for a July 1982 opening. The owners operate another successful restaurant by the same name in Stockton. The new restaurant features dining in the glass-enclosed atrium right on the harbor, or in the main dining room which is accented with hand-carved oak work, fine waterfowl art and pictures of the historic Delta during Tuleberg days.

Fresh fish is sold over the counter beginning at 9 a.m. Lunch starts daily at 11 a.m. with continuous service through dinner to 10 p.m. The cocktail lounge stays open till ? The Fish Market's clam chowder is widely acclaimed. There's cioppino every Friday and a Sunday brunch 10 a.m. to 3 p.m. The menu includes grilled fish, seafood sautees, calamari, steamed clams, crab and shrimp Louies, hot crab sandwiches and even locks and bagels. Guest docking with electricity.

Giusti's, (916) 776-1808, is at the juncture of the Mokelumne's North Fork and Snodgrass Slough near Walnut Grove and is one of the Delta's oldest restaurants. Although the outside of the building appears somewhat ramshackle, inside you find the warmth and neatness you'd expect in an Italian restaurant. Food is good, priced right and in bountiful quantities. There is a palatable inexpensive house wine. Dinner fare includes everything from raviolis and veal cutlets to jumbo prawns.

A special daily luncheon from 11:30 a.m. to 1:30 p.m. (2 p.m. weekends) includes wine. The bar is adjacent to the restaurant and is an active place frequented by locals. Its walls are lined with autographed photos of well-known persons who have visited the place. Brunch is served summer Sundays outside on the new deck and includes such delicacies as bluepoint oysters. Giusti's is closed every Monday and the months of January and February. Dinner service is 5 to 10 p.m., to 11 p.m. Saturdays, and 4 to 10 p.m. Sundays. No dinners Tuesday and Wednesday October to Memorial Day. Guest docking w/electricity.

Happy Harbor, (916) 777-6575, on the San Joaquin near Light #42, just below the Mokelumne, sits up in a two-story building overlooking the broad river. It's active bar is frequented by an enthusiastic boating crowd and there is weekend music and dancing. Daily luncheons 11 a.m. to 2 p.m. offer a steak and prawns combo, steak sandwiches and the popular Fingerlength Hamburger—a 1/3-pounder with fries and salad.

Dinner service is from 6 to 10 p.m. weekdays, till 11 p.m. weekends. Offerings include New Yorks, prawns, steak and lobster, and the favorite steamed clams, which are large cherrystones in copious quantities. The secret clam sauce gets raves, and owner Don Ansel is more than a little proud of his clam chowder. Only top-grade food is used here. Guest docking with electricity.

Harbor Galley, (415) 634-1358, at the new Discovery Bay Yacht Harbor, in "Disco Bay" off Indian Slough. Chef Margo provides informal dining overlooking the water, including six tables on the deck outside for dining *al fresco*, weather permitting. The menu includes fresh mushroom, cheese, ham or combination omelettes, and sandwiches varying from turkey to b.l.t. and steak. There are daily inexpensive luncheon specials such as veal scallopini, open-faced crab sandwiches, the super duper Hoggie-Burger, stuffed filet of sole and traditional German dishes like weiner Schnitzel.

Dinners include steak and lobster, prime rib, New York steaks, jumbo prawns and specials. Desserts feature ice cream and Margo's homemade pies and cheesecake. Sunday brunch features eggs Benedict, usually till 3 p.m. Hours are 11 a.m. to 9 p.m. weekdays, 7 a.m. to 9 p.m. weekends. Winter hours 11 a.m. to 8 p.m. weekdays, 9 a.m. to 8 p.m. weekends. Guest docking w/elect. Catering for special parties.

Hatch Cover, (209) 478-4341, at Stockton's Village West Marina on Fourteenmile Slough, is a modern structure overlooking the water. Its active bar (weekday happy hours) includes a patio deck and is decorated with seafaring photos and artifacts. The restaurant has a reputation for consistently good food, with dinner service only starting at 6 p.m. nightly, 5 p.m. Sundays.

Selection at the salad bar is outstanding, and includes soup and French bread. The menu features filet mignon, teriyaki, beef kabobs, Hawaiian chicken and even a vegetable casserole. You can have rack of lamb, prime rib while it lasts, swordfish, scampi and Alaskan king crabs that look to be critters formidable enough to crawl away with the table. Desserts include cheesecake, turtle pie and ice cream. Entertainment some evenings, guest dock with electricity.

Lighthouse Resort, (916) 777-5236, on the Mokelumne downriver from Hwy 12 bridge, is a bright comfortable place with a new deck extending out over the water. Breakfasts include a variety of omelettes, steak and eggs and other offerings. Luncheons include hamburgers, chicken-burgers, grilled cheese and other sandwiches.

For dinners there's New York steak, the seafood platter, prawns, scallops and fried chicken. Summer hours are 7 a.m. to 9 p.m., to 10 p.m. weekends, winter 7 a.m. to 7 p.m., depending on weather. Beer and wine only. This place has been completely renovated and very well done. Guest docking with electricity.

Lost Isle, (209) 465-6649, on the Stockton Deepwater Channel at Light #24, is a rustic island Shangri-la accessible only by boat. It is not fancy here, but the food is good and you have a good time eating it. Silverware is plastic and you eat off cardboard plates. Cable reels serve as tables and you sit on logs. Peacocks, rabbits and other animals roam the island.

You can get something to eat any time of the day here. Breakfasts include hot cakes, bacon, sausage or ham and eggs and other dishes. Hamburgers and cheeseburgers are nourishing for lunch and during the summer tacos, burritos, enchiladas and chili verdes are served. Dinners offer the 12-ounce ribeye steak with salad, baked potato and wine, plus Mexican dinners during the summer. Open seven days, 7 a.m. to 11:30 p.m. (bar open to 2 a.m.) summers, shorter hours winters. Guest docking with electricity.

Moore's Riverboat, (916) 777-6545, on the Mokelumne just a short distance up from the San Joaquin, has been a solid Delta favorite since its gangways were dropped in 1965. John Moore presides over this floating 156-foot riverboat like a true captain. As well he should, for it took him all of five years to transform the grubby old freighter *Sutter* into this gleaming vessel.

Moore's is dependable. The bar opens every morning at 6 a.m. with breakfasts by 8 o'clock. There is a complete luncheon menu, including inexpensive sandwiches. Dinner fare varies from lobster to Delta crawdads, a Riverboat specialty. You can get something to eat here at any hour of the day till 11 p.m. Weekend entertainment, overnight guest docking with electricity.

P.J.'s At Courtland Docks, (916) 775-2141, in the pear town of Courtland on the east bank of the Sacramento. Sunday brunch is a favorite here, 10 a.m. to 3 p.m., served on the tree-shaded deck in good weather, inside the rest of the time. Includes champagne, choice of five kinds of omelettes, eggs Benedict, waffles, a fruit salad bar and more.

Lunches include five kinds of hamburgers, assorted sandwiches, daily weekday specials such as corned beef and cabbage and other selections. Dinners

Delta crawdads are featured at Cap'n John Moore's Riverboat

include steaks, chicken, scampi, prime rib on weekends and always some kind of fish. Continuous daily service (but closes 3 p.m. Sundays) from 11 a.m. to 9 p.m., 10 p.m. Fridays and Saturdays, closes about an hour earlier winter weekdays, closed Mondays during the winter. Beer and wine only. Guest docking with electricity.

Payter's, (209) 957-3279, at Stockton's Village West Marina on Fourteenmile Slough, has excellent fare at rock-bottom prices. Facilities are clean but not fancy and modest in size. Plastic silverware, Styrafoam plates. Plenty of variety. The breakfast menu has seven types of three-egg omelettes and offers side orders of cornbread or blueberry muffins. There's a wide choice of sandwiches, including turkey, crab salad and steak.

You can get beef burritos, tapatias and beef enchiladas. There's chicken in a basket, shrimp tempura and scallops, crab or shrimp salads and homemade chili—even Pee Wee Burgers for the kids. On nice days, you can take your food to picnic tables outside. You can call ahead for takeout orders to maybe eat on the boat. Open 7 a.m. to 9 p.m. every day, till 11 p.m. summers, beer and wine. Guest docking with electricity.

Petas is situated in the new Grocers Warehouse building at Waterfront Yacht Harbor at the Channel head in Stockton, scheduled for a July 1982 opening. Dubbed "a bit of Europe in good ol' Stockton" it is presided over by the very European Peta himself. Cuisine here is German and features such favorites as Schnitzel, bratwurst, Swedish meatballs with hot potato salad and red cabbage, beef rouladen, sauerbraten and more.

You can have an inexpensive Danish open-faced liver pate or a special soup and sandwich combination for a modest sum, then top it off with a cup of Peta's special blend coffee and a piece of apple strudel. The place includes a bar with live music nightly. Luncheon is from 11 a.m. to 2 p.m., dinner service daily. Guest docking with electricity.

The Point, (707) 374-5400, on the Sacramento River at Delta Marina just below Rio Vista, is one of the prettiest restaurants on the Delta. Inside, all is done in pale blue and it looks bright and inviting. In the entry is posted a schedule of the freighters due to pass. And when one passes, details of its flag, port of origin, destination, cargo and tonnage are broadcast over the public address system. Diners have a good view of the river traffic outside.

At the bar, nifty drinks like the fresh strawberry daiquiri are enticing. Luncheon is served daily from 11 a.m. to 5 p.m. and on Sunday there is the special buffet brunch from 10 a.m. to 12:30 p.m. Daily moderately priced offerings include a crab meat sandwich and a variety of Florentine casseroles. Dinner is served 5 p.m. to 10 p.m. weekdays, till 11 p.m. Saturdays and from noon to 10 p.m. Sundays. The menu is heavy on seafoods with such as sauteed fresh Pacific oysters. But there is a wide choice of other foods also, like Hawaiian chicken and bacon-wrapped filet mignon. Entertainment some weekends, guest docking (with

electricity at Delta Marina). Closed Mondays.

Riverview Lodge, (415) 757-2272, on the Sacramento River in Antioch, has one of the most varied seafood menus to be found anywhere. And at moderate prices. You can have sturgeon or cioppino, and about everything in between.

Of course, you can also get sandwiches, steaks and other beef dishes. Riverview is open every day from at least 11 a.m. till 11:30 p.m., later weekends. You can have breakfast, lunch or dinner and cocktails. Both diners and bar patrons are afforded an excellent view of the river. Overnight guest dock. (Most rental houseboats are not permitted below the Antioch bridge).

Rusty Porthole, (415) 684-2105, at Boyd's Harbor on Bethel Island, overlooks the waters of Piper Slough, with a view of Franks Tract and beyond. Service is seven days per week here for 11 months, closed weekdays in January. Breakfasts include such as the Big Break Breakfast or an omelette concocted from the leftovers of the day before. The dinner menu includes scampi, and other offerings from the sea, plus New York steaks, pork ribs, chicken and specials of the evening. Beer and wine license only.

Dinners are served Fridays and Saturdays all year and other days during the season. This is a pleasant place sprinkled with antiques. There are special meeting rooms and a group barbecue area. Prices are moderate. Plenty of guest docking, with electricity.

Ryde Hotel, (916) 776-1908, graces the banks of the Sacramento River in the hamlet of Ryde between Walnut Grove and Isleton. The old hotel has 50 rooms, and in the downstairs Speakeasy there's a separate rock and roll extravaganza Friday and Saturday April through

Giusti's is one of the Delta's oldest restaurants.

December. But all is calm and peaceful in the upstairs dining area with a contemporary duo with music for listening and dancing, Thur., Fri. and Sat. The Sunday brunch, 9 a.m. to 1 p.m., has a 20-foot table ladened with fresh fruits, sweet rolls, salads and other delicacies. With this you combine a choice of huevos rancheros, eggs Benedict, strawberry crepes, prime rib sandwiches, etc., plus all the champagne you wish.

Breakfasts include nine kinds of omelettes of which the most popular is the "eggstravaganza". For lunch there is a variety of sandwiches, crab or shrimp Louies, and more. Dinners offer veal Oscar, Alaskan king crab (1¼ lb. servings), prime rib Fri. and Sat., scampi and more. Try the jumbo onion rings done in beer batter.

Hours are 11 a.m. to 10 p.m. Tues. - Thur., 7 a.m. to 11 p.m. Fri. and Sat., 7 a.m. to 10 p.m. Sun., open weekends only Jan. - Apr. Cocktail lounge, private dining rooms, catering for special parties. Guest docking.

Spindrift, (916) 777-6654, on the lower San Joaquin just up from Sevenmile Slough, is situated in the top floor of a two-story building, affording you a fine view of the water and the flat farmlands of the big Andrus Island. The bar is tastefully decorated in a nautical motif. Weekend music for dancing and listening by Jack and Christi Lewis. The place has a well-earned reputation for consistently excellent food at fair prices.

The Sunday chicken and dumplings (now also served Wednesdays and Thursdays when open) attracts boaters from around the Delta. Beware, this is doggie-bag territory. Proportions of everything are immense and you can always look forward to a second repast back at the boat. Luncheon is served Saturday and Sunday only. The dinner menu is complete, with a variety of meat and fish dishes. The veal Oscar is outstanding and the stuffed sole is popular. Spindrift is open Wednesday through Sunday, late May through Labor Day, and Friday through Sunday the rest of the year, closed four weeks after New Year's. Guest docking with electricity.

Steamboat Landing, (916) 775-1121, on the Sacramento River at the Steamboat Slough bridge. Sandwiches include eight varieties of hamburgers, deviled egg, fishwich, the Steamboat Dog, fried chicken filet and even peanut butter and jelly. You can get fish and chips, clam strips and fried chicken. Fare includes homemade clam chowder, chili and a soup of the day. Huevos rancheros are served every Saturday and Sunday.

Dinners are served at least Fri., Sat. and Sun. year round, offering chicken, ribs, fish, steak and other dishes. There's a salad bar in the summer. Open seven days, all year. The cocktail lounge is a lively place, a deli (includes pizza) replaces the old grocery store. Guest docking with electricity.

The Store, (916) 777-6562, at Vieira's Resort on the Sacramento River just below Isleton. Atmosphere is informal and brothers Mike and Ron Forthun slant the menu toward seafood with such as mahi mahi, red snapper, lobster and fish and chips. Dinners include teriyaki steak, beef kabobs, veal and more. There are also dinner specials such as fried chicken, scampi and veal dishes. Lunches include 15 offerings of hamburgers, sandwiches and daily specials such as Swiss steak and meatloaf. There's clam chowder and a soup of the day. Breakfasts are hearty and include omelettes as well as the usual fare. Open all year with continuous service from 6:30 a.m. to 11 p.m., closed Mondays. Beer and wine only, guest docking.

Terminous Tavern and Restaurant, (209) 369-1041, at Tower Park Marina on Little Potato Slough at Hwy 12. A fine restaurant situated in one of the rugged old produce sheds that line the slough. Includes one of the prettiest cocktail lounges on the Delta, and you can dine overlooking the water. Open 7 a.m. all year. Breakfasts include seven kinds of omelettes, French toast, hot cakes, fresh fruit in season and other "Individual Dawdlings".

Luncheon fare is such as a variety of hamburgers, a French dip, soup of the day, chef's salad, the "asparaus shed delight" salad and more. Ice cream here. Dinner service starts at 5 p.m. and runs to 11 p.m. summers, 10 p.m. winters, maybe 9 p.m. winter weekdays. Food includes prime rib weekends, beef & chicken kabob combo, steak, top 'n bottom and fresh fish every night. Bar

specializes in bloody Marys with a secret ingredient and fetching fizzes. Summer weekend entertainment. Roomy guest dock with electricity.

Tiki Lagun, (209) 941-8975, is located on Turner Cut and now sports a comfortable (petite) cocktail lounge. Dining is casual but fun here. The big happening here Fridays and Saturdays is the outside barbecue, 7 p.m. till ?, April into October, depending on the weather. It's a laid-back affair. You can dine on the patio deck, out at the picnic tables, or inside. Fare includes 22-ounce steaks, ribs, chicken, catfish fries along with corn-on-the-cob, French fries or beans and the salad bar.

The cafe serves breakfast and hot and cold sandwiches for lunch, 7 a.m. to 6 p.m. seven days summers, then Friday through Mondays 9 a.m. to 6 p.m. winters. Guest docking with electricity.

Tony's Place, (916) 776-1317, in Walnut Grove just across from the merchants courtesy dock on the Sacramento River, has a solid well-deserved reputation and dinner reservations are recommended. Tony and his wife Mary are enthusiastic restaurateurs. They dish out over 2,000 pounds of their special Portuguese beans annually. Tony cuts his own New York steaks, of which approximately 325 will be consumed on a typical summer weekend.

Dinners are served only on Saturday (6 p.m. to 11 p.m.) and Sundays (4 p.m. to 9 p.m.) and there is no printed menu to fuss over. The fare consists solely of New Yorks and veal. Weekday luncheons (11 a.m. to 2 p.m.) are enticing and Tony is proud of his special stew. Tony's is normally closed the last two weeks in September. Overnight guest dock.

The Warehouse restaurant is situated in the new Grocers Warehouse building at Waterfront Yacht Harbor at the Chan-

Stockton's new Waterfront Yacht Harbor may ultimately have six or more restaurants in Grocers Warehouse building. Here, a cruise ship stops in at the harbor's guest dock.

nel head in Stockton, scheduled for a July 1982 opening. It is patterned after a highly successful operation with the same name at Marina del Rey and features an international menu. It occupies a grand amount of space on two floors, with a downstairs cocktail lounge and oyster bar with special drinks such as the "warf wrat". Entertainment nightly.

The "Inventory" consists of such as ribs Rangoon, steak Neptune, chicken Colombia and shrimp Malaysia. You can make a meal of soup and salad, try a "split cargo", or venture beef Maui. There are "stolen goods" (daily specials) and fresh fish nightly. Dinner service is 5:30 to 10 p.m. weekdays, till 11 p.m. Friday and Saturday, and 5 p.m. to 10 p.m. Sundays. Weekday luncheon is 11 a.m. to 2:30 p.m. A champagne buffet brunch is served Saturdays and Sundays 10 a.m. to 3 p.m.

Guest docking with electricity.

Wheel House & Inn Tent, (916) 371-7700, at Raley's Landing on the Sacramento River across from Old Sacramento, is a part of the Marina Inn motel. Breakfast, lunch and dinner are served daily year round. For breakfast you have a choice of ten omelettes, eggs Benedict and even Canadian bacon and eggs. Luncheon fare includes a selection of hot sandwiches from the French dip to hot roast beef, plus cold sandwiches, crab or shrimp Louies and the avacodo royal. There are also daily buffet luncheons on the patio.

Dinner fare includes Coquille Saint Jacques, stuffed river trout, halibut veronique, cioppino, plus filet mignon bearnaise and the Marina Duet—broiled Australian lobster and petit filet. There's clam chowder, escargot and other good things, including daily specials. The popular Sunday brunch is served 10 a.m. to 2:30 p.m. outside in the stunning circus-style Inn Tent, which is also available for special banquets. The busy cocktail lounge has weekday happy hours 4 to 6 p.m. with free hors d'oeuvres that includes the likes of steamed clams. Guest docking.

Wimpy's, (209) 794-2544, on the Mokelumne's South Fork just east of Walnut Grove, is a warm friendly establishment with a family atmosphere and good food priced right. Breakfast lunch and dinner service daily, beginning at 9 a.m. weekdays, 8 a.m. weekends. The all-you-can-eat Sunday brunch enjoys great popularity, 10 a.m. to 2 p.m., then dinner service starts. Sandwiches include hamburgers, a hot crab sandwich and a Jalapeno concoction with turkey, ham and cheese. Dinner offerings are such as New York steak, prawns, spaghetti, veal cutlets and prime rib Fridays. There's homemade pies, ice cream and shakes, homemade biscuits and a lively bar with cocktails overlooking the river. Guest docking.

Windmill Cove, (209) 948-6995, on the Stockton Deepwater Channel between Lights #34 and #36, is perched high on the levee affording diners a commanding view of the river traffic outside. It has a lively cocktail lounge and a new second-story terrace up high on pilings. Dinners include New York and ribeye steaks with baked potato, and salad. A luncheon favorite is the Windmill Cove special, a bacon-wrapped hamburger on a French roll that is a meal in itself.

Breakfasts include omelettes, bacon, sausage or ham and eggs, French toast and even homemade biscuits and gravy on occasion. Windmill is open all year, seven days per week. Luncheon-dinner service is seven days during the summer, breakfasts Friday thru Sunday and holidays. Winter restaurant open days, Friday thru Sunday. Guest dock with electricity.

That about does it. Gourmands, of course, are not infallible. And I've probably left out your favorite spot. There is just not room to cover them all. In "downtown" Bethel Island there's Bel Isle Club, Delta Bell, Wanda's Gang Plank and other eateries but a stroll from the water. But they don't have guest docks and a tie-up can be chancy. At Leisure Landing, there's Hatoba Restaurant.

We've left out Calamity Jane's (old Chili Pepper) and the Holiday Inn at Stockton's Channel head because they do not have docking. The Castaway there is closed at this writing.

Also omitted are places that do not offer a dinner menu. But this does not infer that they do not serve fine food. Breakfasts are memorable at Maxine's (at Korth's Pirates Lair). I've enjoyed patty melts at Tracy Oasis, devoured hamburgers at Snack Barge and feasted on chiliburgers at Bean Pot Resort. I've lunched regally at Union Point Resort.

I've gorged on spaghetti at Middle River Inn, had homemade pie at King Island Resort and pancakes at Herman & Helen's. I've munched crawdads at Del's.

If a boater goes hungry in the Delta, you can be sure it is his own fault.

Top. The fabulous new Ox Box Marina on Georgiana. Bottom. Tahitian dancers perform at Tower Park's DeltaFest.

71

9

Outstanding Anchorages

There are skippers who will speak of their favorite anchorages in hushed voices. When asked about locations, they become furtive and give vague and imprecise directions. When conversing with their cohorts on marine radio to set up a rendezvous, they use secret code names for their destinations. They value their anchorage places and don't want them known to the riffraff.

I am reminded of the sailboater who was comfortably ensconced in his boat at anchor in Lost Slough. A stubble fire on The Meadows pasture land made a power-boating group there wary. They pulled up anchors and moved en masse to Lost Slough. There was much shouting back and forth as they all got anchored and rafted together. On came 110 volt gasoline generators and stereos. When one skipper brought out his chainsaw and began trimming tree limbs around his boat, the lone sailboater decided it was time to move on.

Noisy neighbors a quiet anchorage can quickly undo. Although there are many hundreds of good places to anchor in the Delta, a handful of places continue to attract great numbers of boaters. The popular spots are invariably in pleasant surroundings and afford good protection from both wakes and wind. They can be busy, vibrant places during the summer. If you wish to be alone, you best seek out your own anchorage. But you'll surely want to know about the popular ones.

Hog Island

Hardly a romantic name for such a beautiful place. But Hog Island has a few nice anchorages and it is not known well enough to be crowded. It is one of those islands on the San Joaquin that was cut in two when the giant dredges straight-

On the back side of Hog Island.

ened the river to form the Stockton Deepwater Channel.

It is situated across from bustling Lost Isle at Light No. 21. The anchorages are on the southwest portion of the "back side" of Hog and can barely be seen from the river. The northern portion of the island has a few residences and is headquarters for the Weber Point Y.C., so is not suitable for anchoring.

Disappointment Slough

Early riverboat pilots negotiating the old San Joaquin River apparently gifted Disappointment Slough with its negative-sounding name. Navigation was a trifle tougher for them back before the river was straightened. The proud river had its share of wiggles around Disappointment. And on foggy or black moonless nights it was easy for a pilot to confuse this pleasant 5-mile slough for just another bend in the river.

You can understand a skipper's chagrin a few miles later when he discovered he'd been lured off course. During the remainder of the voyage, the "disappointed" skipper would have to suffer the snickers and jibes of crew members anxious to make port.

This slough represents no disappointment for today's boater, however. It is peppered with small islands that provide some very nice anchorages. Its location is handy. Half way up the slough at Honker Cut is King Island Resort with fuel, rental houseboats, groceries and a cafe.

It terminates at the juncture of Bishop Cut and Fourteenmile Slough. Until a few years ago, a cable-drawn ferry at this point shuttled equipment to Rindge Tract, but it was replaced by a high-clearance concrete bridge. Where the three sloughs meet, you'll find the new Paradise Point Marina with rental houseboats, fuel, groceries, a cafe and a complete boat repair yard. This is a growing and deluxe marina complex.

Disappointment has three entrances from the San Joaquin. The down-river pair flank a good-size island that's back side boasts a splendid anchorage with a protective tule berm its entire length. Its neighboring up river island has an inner lake known as "Lost Lake". Some good anchoring spots are to be found around this island. And more than once I've breakfasted on wild berries plucked from its bordering bushes.

Mandeville Tip

The mud-hungry dredges chomped their way through huge Mandeville Island while digging the Stockton Deepwater Channel. When it was over, the mother island hardly noticed the absence of its 175-acre tip. For three decades thereafter, the Tip lay dormant. It became just another of the legions of tule-fringed Delta islands.

But on August 30, 1965 the San Joaquin County Parks Department awakened the slumbering island. They arranged to lease it from the Stockton Port District. They constructed a series of docks around part of the Tip's perimeter. They built barbecues, picnic tables and installed portable toilets and trash bins. They trimmed back the tenacious blackberry bushes to establish a mile-long nature trail.

Dinghying around Mandeville Tip.

Mandeville Tip at 4th of July is an extraordinary happening.

Not in a long time have public funds been so wisely spent. The county transformed Mandeville Tip into an outstanding boat-in island park that is unique in the Delta. The rustic feel of the outdoors was retained. You'll not find electricity, water or other services here. The Tip enjoys a solid popularity.

The early arriver boaters get space at the docks, while the rest have to be content to anchor bow-to beneath the island's trees—no sad fate, to be sure. There is no land access to the island. Workers come in by boat to haul off garbage, empty the portables, and effect repairs.

A major happening here annually is over July 4th when thousands of boats gather for Barron Hilton's gala fireworks display (Hilton is a member of a nearby duck club on Venice Island). Fireworks are shot from a barge in the bay off the Tip. And the whole area is one giant party. The exact date of the fireworks is posted on a sign outside the duck club.

When Proposition 13 was passed, the Parks Dept. decided it did not have sufficient funds to operate Mandeville Tip. The Port of Stockton then graciously took over operation, but found it not always easy to keep up a park with longshoremen trimming weeds, repairing docks, etc. Now the Port and Parks jointly share the task of keeping the park operational.

At this writing, a long seige of wet weather and high water has done considerble damage to the Tip's docks. And it is not clear if there are funds and manpower to make the facility right again. Plus, the Port is uncomfortable with its legal liability position here. Park or not, this will always be a popular place in which to anchor. But it would be a pity to see the whole concept go under, so to speak.

Mandeville Tip is below Light No. 3 on the San Joaquin and there is a rustic sign posted on its river side.

Maybe as many as 3,000 boats assemble around Mandeville Tip for the big 4th of July fireworks display.

Potato Slough

The Delta was graced with few of those salty, seafaring (sometimes pretentious) names. Consider Potato Slough. It most likely got its name because potatoes were at one time such an important Delta crop. There were special riverboats called potato boats built to haul the crop (the decaying remains of one may still be seen across from the Delta Y.C. on Head-reach Cutoff).

Stephens Marine, Stockton's prestigious constructor of $ million-plus yachts, in earlier times built at least 125 fast 26-

foot runabouts they called "spud boats". They were primarily used by potato buyers who had to get around the Delta fast to handle their potato negotiations.

Shima Tract, over by Fourteenmile Slough, was named after George Shima, an early Japanese field worker who went on to become a Delta millionaire. Stockton even crowned him the "Potato King".

Ah, but I degress from the subject of anchorages. The Delta contains both a Potato and a Little Potato slough. And Potato is often referred to as Big Potato. It

Taking it easy anchored on Potato Slough.

feeds off the San Joaquin at Light No. 53, then loops around part of Venice Island to intersect with Little Connection Slough.

It is a wide waterway, but much of its course is divided by tule islands that give boaters almost two distinct routes over it. Two portions of it are popular for anchoring.

The first is in the shelter of a cluster of three islands in about a half mile from the San Joaquin. The largest of the three islands is Fig Island (with a fig tree on it, of course) that has a hideaway cabin and dock owned by a grizzled Stockton yachtsman named Balky. Balky laments the fact that with 1,000 miles of Delta to anchor in, a few demented boatmen like to tie to his private dock. There is plenty of good anchoring space here without trespassing on this tiny patch of private, posted property.

Along with houseboaters and cruiser owners, many sailboaters like Potato. It is here that daring younsters can sometimes be seen dangerously clinging to lines on the end of spinnaker sails wildly flapping in the summer breeze. Great sport—to watch! A string of a half dozen overlapping tule berms farther in on the slough forms many protected coves in which great numbers of boats like to anchor. This can be a festive place.

Five Fingers

Five harbors are cut into a large tule island between Columbia Cut and Connection Slough south of the San Joaquin. They are wide, cut in perhaps 50 yards each and have sufficient water depth. They are secluded and easy to pass without notice. Each can harbor a surprising number of boats, and on fine summer days they are spilling over.

Knowing boaters call the place Five Fingers, although you won't find the name shown on maps or charts. Brush grows high and thick around each finger, adding to the seclusion and deadening sounds from neighboring boats.

It is a cheery place with ominous overtones. Delta lore has it that the Fingers were dug out to serve as secret ports for barges smuggling in illegal Chinese laborers, supposedly to toil the remainder of their lives on the levees and farms. The fact that harbors as large as these are not shown on charts lends credence to the tale for many people. They think the harbor entrances were hidden by movable brush.

Such stories die hard. But I found the explanation in a nearby farmer who has a propensity to turn a fast buck. One time when he had a dredge idle for a few days, he brought it on over and started chomping harbors into this island. His scheme was to lease them out to individuals or clubs. Somewhere, the plan apparently went awry. But some very good harbors remained for us boaters.

"Be sure to tell your readers how to find Five Fingers," ordered Lou Sparrenberger, the River Route mailman. "I'm continually stopped by boaters in that area looking for the place."

Okay, we've marked the chart to include Five Fingers. The island is actually on the waters of Middle River, not far below the big cable ferry mentioned in *The Back Way To Bethel* earlier in this book. Watch out for smugglers.

Lost Slough And The Meadows

Sailboaters long frequented Lost Slough because they could not clear the railroad bridge into The Meadows. And it will be interesting to see if the pattern changes now that this bridge remains open. But Lost Slough doesn't have to take a back seat to any other slough. It can stand on its own merits.

It slips off Snodgrass Slough just before the bridge and runs for a bit over three miles before it is cut off by recent construction on Interstate 5. Its center is strung almost continuously with tule berms that narrow the slough and in effect make it two sloughs with only a couple places to cross over from one side to the other.

There are wide anchorage harbors at its near-90-degree bend and toward its far end. Brush comes in close on this slough and there is a secluded "lost" feel to much of it. Traffic is light as most small boats that are just cruising the area tend to gravitate toward The Meadows, thus taking the pressure off Lost Slough.

The Meadows is more a state of being than just a great anchoring place on the Delta. Its reputation precedes it. And you just naturally approach it in the festive mood. Our boat club visits there each year for its "Meadows Lark" for a nine-day period. And members plan vacations a year in advance to be sure to be free at that time. It is our most popular outing.

Geographically, The Meadows is a 1,400 yard dead-end appendage off Snodgrass Slough. It is a wide 150 yards or so for most of its length and water depths are excellent. Its northwest bank is tree-lined and slopes up gently to levees that are well inland of the water's edge. It is pocked with fine sandy beaches. Boaters can get ashore and there is plenty of room to roam around. Boat-campers pitch tents on the shore.

There is an unwritten no-wake rule in The Meadows that honestly works. And any offenders quickly know about it. Current there is slight. Boaters by the dozens float about on inner tubes and air mattresses. Runabouts shuttle into nearby marinas for supplies. The slough is like Main Street on Saturday night with rubberneckers constantly cruising by. But

This rental houseboat is headed into Lost Slough, near The Meadows. The abandoned railroad bridge is slated for removal.

here they are in boats rather than autos. And they become part of the show.

Next door, you can sometimes hear hot boats blowing out the carbon in the tail-end section of Snodgrass. There, going fast is permitted and it is handy for big-boat people who bring along a small boat for skiing. A few houseboaters anchor here, but wake action is a bother.

There is a friendly spirit to The Meadows and invariably I get to know new people whenever I anchor there. For the hungry, there are berry bushes ashore. Black bass fishing is good here when things slow down after the summer. Always there is talk about The Meadows being turned into a state park. But who would want to change it. It all works out too well the way it is.

Note: *As we go to press, plans call for removal of the unusual railroad bridge on Snodgrass Slough. This will most likely take place in late 1982 or early 1983. Also there is a move afoot to make Snodgrass into a 5 mph or no waterskiing area (along with some other areas) and there are objections to this. Should it come to pass, you will be apprised by signs.*

We found this large craft behind Locke on Dredger Cut.

Steamboat Slough

On summer weekends, a regular floor show is unfolding in the first half mile or so of Steamboat. When I arrive there, I like to cruise up and down the area at least once for a look at all the goings on. Boats anchor here on the west bank. The custom is to anchor parallel to the shore. The current is strong and the slough is not sufficiently wide for bowing in big boats with anchors hazardly out past mid-stream.

There is a long sandy beach off the side of Steamboaters. Parked there is a regular flotilla of dinghies. They belong to anchored boatmen on the opposite bank who dinghy over to use the beach. Formerly they would stroll up the hill for libations at Steamboaters. But the resort has gone through a succession of pro-prietorships and there are no indications that it will open for the summer of 1982. Too bad, for it is a pretty place and some good times have been had there.

However, Steamboat Landing, just above the bridge, has had new life breathed into it and is becoming the in place to go. It now has cocktails year round, food, sundries and other supplies. The sandy beach (fee for use) at the base of the drawbridge is part of this operation and is aswarm with bathers on summer weekends.

There are families that have been summering in this part of Steamboat for three generations. Here and there farther down the slough there are inviting places to anchor. But it is all happening up here on that first stretch off the Sacramento. And there is no cover charge for the show.

10

Outwitting The Fish

Delta waters are inhabited by a surprising variety of fish, ranging from the ubiquitous catfish to the mighty sturgeon. There are striped bass, largemouth bass, crappie, bluegill, shad, salmon and others. Most any time of the year, some kind of Delta fish is bound to be biting. And for a change of pace, you can even trap tasty crawdads.

Striped Bass

Old "pin-stripes", as the striped bass is fondly called, is the most sought after fish in the Delta. And it is estimated that the present population of the fish in legal size (18 inches and over) is in the order of 1.5 to 2 million. The annual catch in California is around 300,000.

Originally there were no striped bass in California. They were first introduced here in 1879 when 132 small bass were brought here by rail from New York and released near Martinez. A second planting of 300 was made in the lower Suisun Bay in 1882. They proliferated and within 10 years of the original planting, the commercial catch of the fish averaged 1,000,000 pounds per year. Commercial fishing of the stripers was outlawed in 1932.

The fish goes to 65 pounds and over. At a Delta bass fishing derby, some time ago, the top three places went to anglers with bass over 50 pounds. Although a more typical keeper might be 10 pounds or so. Stripers are anadromous, living part of their life in the sea, but returning each season to spawn in the Delta's San Joaquin and Sacramento rivers.

Anglers eagerly await the spawning run in April, May and June when fishing is at its best. A second run occurs in the fall, from sometime in September running through the end of the year and later. Trolling with lures or baitfishing are the most common methods of pursuing the striper.

Bait varies somewhat by area. In the lower Delta grass shrimp and whole bullheads are used. When using bullheads, one can be sure that if he catches anything, it will be big in size. Farther up in the Delta,

cut-bait like sardines and anchovies is popular.

Some anglers reverse the bait on the hook turning the fleshy side out to appeal to the striper's keen sense of smell. Threadfin shad is also very effective Delta bait.

You bait fish near the bottom with 3/0 to 5/0 hooks rigged on sliding sinkers so that the fish can move off with the bait without feeling any pull against it. As a rule there is more fishing action when the tides are switching. During a flood tide the fish is confused and moving about aimlessly and is apt to take anything.

Trolling with deep-diving plugs can be successful and the angler strives to troll into a school of stripers. You troll at maybe three to five mph. Some fishermen drift with the tide a portion of the time.

If you are a stranger to the Delta, the proprietor of one of the local bait shops will be your best friend. He is right up to date on what is being caught, where and on what kind of bait or lure. He is invaluable to you. And he will be stocking the bait that is most effective in his area. Favored equipment is spinning rods 5 foot to maybe 7½ foot in length with 20 to 25 pound test line.

Striper season is open all year, minimum length is 18 inches and the daily bag limit is two fish, with of course only that number in possession.

Tips From An Expert:

Bait fishing techniques. Taking striped bass on light tackle can be fun. Basic tackle should include a medium rod with a fast tip and a spinning reel or bait-casting reel. Line should be approximately 20 lb. test with a sliding sinker rig plus a 40 in. long snelled leader with a 5/0 to 9/0 hook (depending on size of bait).

After you have made your cast, sit back and relax and wait for the action. Upon seeing the rod tip dip somewhat, drop the tip of the rod toward the water, put reel on free spool, and wait for a slight tug. When this happens, release the line and let the fish run with the bait.

When it looks like he has the bait, put the

reel in gear and wait until the rod tip arcs downwards and the line is tight. Now set the hook with some authority and watch out for some good healthy runs.

Best baits to use are threadfin shad, anchovies, sardines, bloodworms and pile worms. I find shad the best. *Jay Sorensen, founder California Striped Bass Assn., owner Jolly's Bait & Sports Shop.*

Tips From An Expert:

Trolling Techniques: There are waters in the Delta in which you can troll successfully year round. But water must be clear enough for the fish to see the lure, even though the lure also puts out vibrations the fish can feel. When winter water is muddy, I have more success in shallower (clearer water) places with light current such as Franks Tract, Big Break, Sherman Lake and the back sloughs.

Equipment I like is medium-light tackle, 7½ ft. to 8½ ft. rod with very light action, and a level-wind reel similar to the Ambassador 7000, rigged with 375 yards minimum of 17 or 20-lb. test line such as Stren monofiliment with leaders made from the same material. Some trollers prefer wire spreaders with huskier leaders. To avoid losing striking fish, set reel drag light. Check new lures to see that action is proper at trolling speeds. Continuously check your snaps and look for frayed leaders, especially after each fish. If in doubt, replace.

I rig off a three-way swivel with 15 inches of leader with a snap swivel to a jig (such as the Bugeye) and a 36-in. leader to a snap swivel to a lure such as the Rebel or the Rapala. Length can vary with different size poles. I put a trailing rubber worm on the jig. Use light-colored lures light days, dark-colored dark days.

Most often, the fish are laying close to the bottom. And that's where you must troll your lures. If you are not losing occasional lures to snags, then you are not trolling close enough to the bottom. You have to "feel the bottom". Watch your rod tip, and if it is not dipping from time to time, let out more line. When it does start to dip (from hitting bottom) take in just enough line to stop it. Obviously, the more you know about the bottom in the areas you fish, the better you'll get. Soon you'll learn how much line to let out to fish at various depths.

To be proficient, a good depthfinder is a must. Some are very sensitive and with them you can spot fish and pinpoint their depth (I use a Loran #2460 Bluewater Pro). I troll at maybe three to five mph, depending on lures. If I'm trolling in say 20 feet of water and spot fish on the finder at say 15 feet, then I reel in enough line to be trolling then at that depth.

When a fish strikes, don't panic. You've got plenty of time to work the fish as long as the boat stays in motion. Turn off the reel's "clicker" to save wear and tear on your equipment.

Never, but never, let the line go slack. And never "thumb" the reel or tighten the drag. Given slack, a fish that has taken the jig will spit it out. Fish that have slaped at the lure will often be caught on the side of the face. Thumbing or a tight drag will tear the fragile flesh loose.

Bring in all other poles in the boat to get them out of the way. After the boat is in neutral, start reeling the fish in. If the tide is working against you, the boat driver may have to move the boat in the direction of the fish to help you retrieve line.

Have a large landing net ready. If you are fighting a large fish, try to tire him out and bring him in belly up. Keep the fish in the water and put the landing net under him. Stun the fish with a small club (I use the cut off back of a pool cue) so that he doesn't flop around in the boat and drive hooks into you. I like to keep the fish in a cooler with fresh water rather than chancing losing him on a stringer.

When fishing shallower water in the winter, I rig without the jig and use a shallow-diving lure, rather than a deep-diver. This also lets you troll closer to the boat when conditions are crowded with other anglers after the same school of fish. *Larry Reedy, owner and guide, Delta Fish Finders charters.*

Tips From An Expert:

Stockton Turning Basin Techniques. Generally the spring run (April into July) produces smaller fish than in the fall. And many stripers are landed both from boats and from the bank. Boaters troll or drift live threadfin shad which are hand netted in the early morn along the bank. Trollers use the deep-diving Rebel and weighted jig combination. These are trolled 20 to 40 yards behind the boat and are effective when fish are schooled in the area.

Live bait fishermen either anchor and fish on the bottom or drift slowly with electric motors with 25 to 30 feet of line out, with a small weight to get the line near the bottom. Plug casting toward shore is also effective. Productive areas are the "wine slip" (the large slip in the Port where great quantities of wine was once shipped), north bank of the Port, mouth of the San Joaquin along the ore docks, off the old Pollock Shipyards, uptown off Harrison St. and into McLeod Lake and even right up to Center St.

The fall run produces larger fish, mostly with trolled Rebels or anchored with dead shad as bait. Shad run along the banks during their spring spawning run only and in the winter must be taken with a hand dip net out in deeper water. They can be found in schools with a depthfinder. *Jack Gordon, past president California Striped Bass Assn.*

Best Areas: For boat fishing: Sherman Lake when the water depth is less than five feet; the power lines on the Sacramento River within two hours of low tide and two-hours of high tide (fish the incoming tide); Threemile Slough where it empties into the Sacramento River and where it empties into the San Joaquin River; Decker Island—on the Sacramento River on the west side of the island, on the north end of the island near the entrance to Threemile Slough, and on the south side of the island near the pilings; the dairy located approximately a mile and a half north of the Brannan Island SRA park entrance on the east side of the Sacramento River (look for a sandy beach with some trees—fish about fifty yards offshore and south of the beach about half to three-quarters of a mile), Franks Tract SRA, Middle and Old Rivers, San Andreas shoals on the San Joaquin, White Slough,

the Mokelumne River from the San Joaquin to Hwy 12 and near the Cross Delta Channel.

For bank fishing: Both sides of the Sacramento River at the Rio Vista bridge; on Sherman Island Road next to the power lines; on Highway 160 north of Brannan Island SRA to Isleton and beyond; on Twitchell Island Road next to Sevenmile Slough; on Brannan Island Road from Jackson Slough Road to Highway 12; public fishing piers at Rio Vista, Antioch and Antioch Bridge; San Joaquin River near Lt. #32; Old River near the San Joaquin and Middle River on Bacon Island Road.

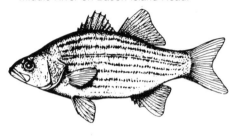

TYPICAL LINE HOOK UP/ Sliding Sinker with Sleeve

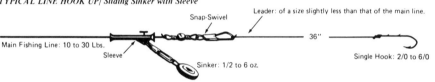

Snap-Swivel

Leader: of a size slightly less than that of the main line.

Main Fishing Line: 10 to 30 Lbs.

Sleeve

Sinker: 1/2 to 6 oz.

36"

Single Hook: 2/0 to 6/0

TYPICAL LINE HOOK UP/ Trolling with Jig & Lure

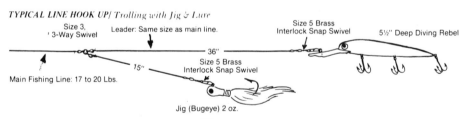

Size 3, 3-Way Swivel

Leader: Same size as main line.

Size 5 Brass Interlock Snap Swivel

5½" Deep Diving Rebel

36"

15"

Size 5 Brass Interlock Snap Swivel

Main Fishing Line: 17 to 20 Lbs.

Size 5 Brass Interlock Snap Swivel

Jig (Bugeye) 2 oz.

Sturgeon

The sturgeon is the largest fresh-water fish in the world. The white sturgeon is the specie commonly caught in the Delta. It reaches a length of 20 feet and a weight of 1,000 pounds. One was recorded as weighing 1,900 pounds. In earlier times, they were hauled from Delta waters with mule teams.

The fish is a slow grower and some reach an age of 100 years. Its mouth is on the underside of its head and is extended purse like to suck up small pieces of food. This is a vacuum cleaner kind of action and a sturgeon in Idaho's Snake River was reported to have eaten a half bushel of onions it found floating in the river. It is a fearsome-looking fish, very often larger than

the fishermen in quest of it.

In the 1870s it was commercially caught in great numbers, but soon began to disappear. In 1901 the season was closed for eight years. It was reopened in 1910 but again closed in 1917. Sport fishing for sturgeon became legal in 1954. Most every year a good number are caught in the Delta weighing over 200 pounds, with many many weighing somewhat less. After a tagging program in 1968, the Calif. Dept. of Fish and Game estimated the keepable white sturgeon population at 114,000 with an annual catch of about seven percent. That amounts to an impressive catch of almost 8,000!

Most sturgeon are caught bait fishing.

81

Ghost or grass shrimp are considered best, but the fish will take shad minnows, crayfish, and other baits. A medium-to-heavy-weight rod with sensitive tip and a conventional bait casting reel is probably most common, though many people use spinning reels. Use a 30- to 50-pound-test line with wire leaders and single or double hooks, and a sliding sinker setup. They strike hard and it is not unusual to take several hours landing a big one. A cable noose is used to boat the fish.

Usually the best season is from the be-ginning of winter when the water starts to get muddy, until early summer. On the Sacramento River prime areas are the Decker Island entrance to Threemile Slough, off the old dairy, the Rio Vista bridge, and the Isleton bridge. San Pablo and Suisun Bay and the mothball fleet are superb areas. Cache Slough and off Liberty Island are good. They are taken on Old River and on the San Joaquin River near Fourteenmile and Sevenmile Slough.

Bag limit is one daily and one in posses-sion. Minimum size is 40 inches.

TYPICAL LINE HOOK UP/ Sliding Sinker without Sleeve

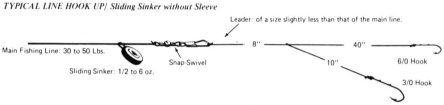

Black Bass

The largemouth black bass is the fight-ingist fish in the Delta system. Until recently this fish has been neglected by many Delta anglers. But suddenly black bass fishing has become the in thing to do. There are contests with big dollar prizes. And they have spawned an elite field of professional bass fishermen who make their living com-peting in these contests and through tackle endorsements.

The modern bass boat is capable of maybe 50 mph and is gadget ridden. These anglers don't leave anything to chance. Their contests are held regularly in the Delta and it is fun to watch the eager anglers speed off in search of their fighting fish. Usually a few fish in the catch will go to over five pounds. But fish in the order of two pounds or so are more common. Although an 11½-pounder was caught in Snodgrass Slough.

To their credit, most of these competition sportsmen return their catch live to the water.

The warmer months are usually best fish-ing, July through September. Black bass prefer waters up to 72 deg. and spawn in the spring when the water temperature exceeds 50 degrees.

The black bass is a structure fish, that is that he prefers to hang out around rocks, tree stumps, brush on even sunken auto-mobiles. This means he is found in close to shore. He'll hit your lure hard and in an instant take it home with him if you will let him. This means you have to be alert to the strike or you'll lose a lot of tackle and fish.

Lures are prefered, both deep-diving and surface lures. Some surface lures are crank-baits, spinnerbaits, plastic worms and jigs. Although you can bait fish using live min-nows, nightcrawlers, red worms, or crayfish with a bobber and some shot sinkers to hold the bait down. But even with this, fish in close to the shore where the fish are most apt to be.

A good rod of 5½ to 6½ feet is preferred, with a good grade reel with full ball bearing construction, excellent drag setup and a five-to-one ratio. The fish is not fond of fast water, so you find him in the deadend sloughs and around inlets. He'll be found at rocky points or brushy areas in most sloughs such as Threemile, Georgiana, Steamboat, Miner Hog, Beaver, Sycamore, White, Lost, Snodgrass, Rock, Indian, Four-teenmile and others, as well as Franks Tract and Sherman Lake.

Fishing will be somewhat better in the mornings and evenings. Bag limit is five daily and in possession. Minimum size is 12 inches.

Catfish
Are Dependable

The catfish is thought of as the be-whiskered darling of the Delta, for he bites year round and is a pushover for the tyro angler. It is a delicious eating fish. The catfish's numbers are legion. Some four million are annually caught in California and the Delta is a top source.

There are at least four varieties of catfish inhabiting the Delta. Of these, the white catfish is by far the most prevalent. It averages around nine inches in length. But Delta channel cats weighing over five pounds are routinely caught, especially in the cooler months. A while back, a 27-pounder was taken by a youngster at Windmill Cove.

At one time the Delta supported a thriving catfish industry. Old river rats lived in houseboats along the river, or in shanties that clung to the levee banks. They depended on the catfish for their very existence. And when they ran out of money they went fishing.

The fish were cleaned and packaged in Delta fishing camps, such as the one that existed on Burns Cutoff near Stockton, then shipped to Bay Area markets. Catfish graced the menus of some of the very best restaurants then. But commercial fishing for catfish was terminated in 1953.

The catfish hunts his food on the bottom. To catch him rig number four hooks with a leader and a swivel snap for a sinker that will weigh one to three ounces depending on current conditions. He is a nocturnal feeder, so you will usually catch more after dark or by fishing in shady spots. Although I regularly see stringersful caught during the day.

He is not a particularly picky eater. Although fresh water clams are his favorite, he is content to dine on cut pieces of sardines or anchovies, grass shrimp or worms. A friend of mine, John Wiselogel, swears by Vienna sausages as bait.

One night John and I were hurriedly summoned from a river joint bar because he obviously had something big on his line, which he'd left in the water. It was a giant of a cat. John didn't have a landing net (you worry about having one for stripers, but not particularly for cats) and worried about

losing the fish trying to bring it into his cruiser. I got his waste basket and tried to use it as a landing net. It didn't work and we lost that giant cat. John felt bad. But next week he arrived with a landing net—and a new supply of Vienna sausages.

Catfishing is a lazy sport. You toss out the line and take up the slack. Let the rod rest on the rail of the boat. When its tip starts moving, grab the rod and set the hook.

Those harmless-looking whiskers (called barbels) on a catfish can prick you and cause swelling of the hand if you are allergic to them. They are used by the catfish to taste and feel. The catfish may not be very handsome, but he's handy to have around.

Bag limit is 20 daily and in possession. No size limit.

Tips From An Expert:

Patience, movement, light tackle, variety of baits. Follow these four suggestions and you should catch fish. Catfish don't always bite when you want, so you have to wait 'em out. Don't be afraid to move ten yards or a half mile. Catfish tend to "school up". If you don't get a bite in a 20 to 30 minute period, don't hesitate to move to another spot.

I recommend light tackle, no greater than 12-pound-test for cats. You can always play the fish if it's a lunker. Both sliding sinkers and the regular setup are effective. I like the regular setup in Delta waters (weight at end of the line, and two hooks above the weight, each about 12 inches apart).

I suggest you stay with one bait. Personally, I think clams catch more catfish than any other bait in these waters. But don't wait too long to switch to something else if you are not getting "hits". Sardine pieces, chicken livers and worms or crawlers all work well. In my book the fun of fishing catfish is only the beginning . . . the real fun and enjoyment is in the eating. Better than trout any day. *Bel Lange, from Bel Lange's Outdoorsman.*

TYPICAL LINE HOOK UP/ Fixed Sinker/Sinker on Bottom

Leader: of a size slightly less than that of the main line.

8″ — 16″ — 15″

10″ — 10″

Snap-Swivel   Snap-Swivel

Sinker: 1/2 to 6 oz.

Main Fishing Line: 8 to 15 Lbs.   No. 2 Hooks

Other Delta Fish

American Shad make two spawning runs in the Delta beginning in May and excellent fishing may extend into July. Bump-netting shad is done at night on the Mokelumne River from about Hwy 12 to the Cosumnes. You use a conicle-shaped net with an 8 ft. handle, out of an outboard-powered boat. You drag the net in the water as the boat moves slowly. When you feel a "bump", you heave the fish into the boat. Shad are also caught in the Sacramento River from below Sacramento to Red Bluff. Shad fishermen use fly rods or a spinning outfit with six to eight pound monofiliment. Preferred lures are tiny "shad darts" or leadhead jigs. Limit is 25 fish and sometimes the action is fast, indeed.

Salmon are taken in the Sacramento, Cache Slough and Steamboat Slough by knowing anglers. A few salmon are taken in the San Joaquin and Mokelumne River systems. **Crappie** are taken year round and can go to well over two pounds. They prefer the cover of bushy shores and are most often found in the Delta's dead-end sloughs. They are caught on minnows, feathered jigs and even on flies.

Bluegills, Sacramento pike and other panfish are routinely taken bait fishing. Your chances of catching such fish off most any dock in the Delta are good. **Carp** can go to 20 pounds and more, but is considered a trash fish by many anglers. But some prefer this bony fish and it is often smoked (as is shad, also a bony fish). Most of the fish you see surfacing in the Delta are carp and you begin to recognize that flash of gold.

Catchin' Crawdads

Some fishermen think of crawdads only in the bait category. But in truth they are delectable crustaceans served in some of the best restaurants. They are commercially trapped in the Delta. In the past, over half a million pounds were annually shipped from here to Sweden. The Swedes go wild over them, and one of their national festivals focuses on crawdads.

Catching them is easy. You need a good trap and they are sold in Delta shops for around $15. They are made of wire mesh and are cylindrical in shape with funneled openings in each end to allow crawdad access. There is a little trap door in the side through which you place the bait.

If you only plan to do a limited amount of crawdadding, as when on a houseboating vacation, you can buy an inexpensive Gee minnow trap and make do with it by enlarging the hole. Some houseboat firms will rent you a trap. Crawdaders must have a fishing license.

Perforated cans of cheap dog food make fine bait—the cheaper the better, as the crawdads prefer the high cereal content. When you stop for the night, you drop the baited trap overboard by a line and let it rest on the bottom. Next morning you might find 20 to 50 or more crawdads.

Our crustacean is a night feeder, so if you trap during the day do it in a shady spot. You will have best results where the water moves briskly. Although you can depend on trapping some crawdads all year long, the best months are from mid-May to December.

To prepare crawdads, you first purge them by placing them in clean water, then into heavily salted water for five minutes. Then rinse them again in clean water. Bring a pot of water to boil and add a pound of salt. Next add three sliced lemons, two onions, two garlic cloves, Cayenne pepper to taste, and a package of dry seafood boil.

Place five to seven pounds of crayfish in the pot and boil for five minutes. Turn off the fire, cover the pot and let them soak in the mixture for 20 to 30 minutes. Taste one and if seasoning is insufficient, let them soak a bit longer.

To eat, cut off tail portion, peel off the shell and dip in spicy tomato sauce, lemon juice or drawn butter. Meat can also be got from the large claws. Crawdad meat will also do well in most recipes calling for lobster or crab meat.

Besides the names listed under "Tips From An Expert" other fishing information was provided courtesy of Hap's Bait Shop, Monterey Bait Shop and The Trap of Rio Vista, and Bob's Bait Shop of Isleton. Thanks, folks.

Larry and Carole Reedy probably catch as many stipers as anyone in the Delta.

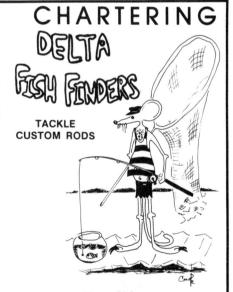
85

11

Stockton—
A Busy Delta Port

On! Somewhere in this favored land the
   sun is shining bright;
The band is playing somewhere, and
   somewhere hearts are light;
And somewhere men are laughing and
   somewhere children shout.
But there is no joy in Mudville—
   mighty Casey has struck out.

The San Francisco Examiner, June 3,
1888 by Ernest Lawrence Thayer.

During its early years, Stockton went
by a number of names. One name that
was particularly descriptive was Mudville.
For during the rainy season the whole
town was a quagmire. And there are men
who steadfastly claim that is was the
Stockton baseball team that inspired
Thayer to write his immortal poem about
the Mudville nine. Maybe so. In any case,
the town's professional baseball team has
adopted the name, the Stockton Mudville
Ports.

The founder of Stockton, Charles
Weber, obtained a land grant with his
partner William Gulnac in 1844 for 48,747
acres in the Stockton and surrounding
area. In 1845 Gulnac sold his interest in
the grant to Weber for $50 worth of
groceries and a $10 white horse. Stockton
for a time was known as Tuleberg because of the tules that grew profusely
along the water's edge, and as Castoria
for the many beavers that were trapped in
the area (*castor* is Spanish for beaver).

The town became legally known as
Stockton in 1850 and was incorporated. It
is believed to be the first town in California with an English name. Until then the
towns received either Spanish or Indian
names. Stockton is apparently a popular
name for there are at least 14 communities in the USA so named. I know from
experience because some of my maga-

zine articles checks once went to Stockton, Texas before they finally found me
here in Mudville.

At first, Weber had difficulties enticing
settlers to his settlement. But all that
changed when gold was discovered. The

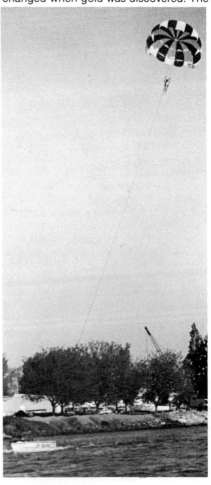

A daring Parasailor on the Channel

87

A crowded and busy harbor at Windmill Cove.

river route through Stockton and then overland became the easiest and quickest route to the southern mines and the town prospered.

It was recorded that 44,000 persons passed through Stockton between April of 1849 and February of 1850. Another problem was of officers and crewmen abandoning their ships in Stockton to head for the mines. Some 14,000 of them are said to have done this during the same 11-month period. The abandoned ships began to clog the channel and were moved to Mormon Slough to be stripped of usable lumber, then burned.

Before the sailboats came, some passengers arrived in Stockton aboard whale boats with San Francisco sailors they'd hired manning the oars. The first steam-powered vessel to arrive was in 1849, probably the side-wheeler *John A. Sutter*. In the following year on a run to Marysville, she exploded and was totally wrecked. Paddlewheelers continued to call on Stockton for over 75 years.

Today, Stockton has considerable to entice the pleasure boater. With a metropolitan population approaching 200,000 it is by far the largest city in the Delta. You can boat right up to the Channel head.

Schmitz Development's $100 million redevelopment project on the south bank of the channel is well underway. Already

completed is its Waterfront Yacht Harbor with berthing, spacious guest docks and other marine facilities. Grand opening for its "Ghirardelli Square" style Grocer's Warehouse was July 4, 1982. It includes a collection of restaurants and shops, making the marina an ideal stopover for one or more days. Ultimately it will include office towers, condomimiums and other shops.

From here, towntown is but a stroll away. There are two handy motels. The Chinese influence is evident in the area's restaurants. Several street signs are even in Chinese. The Stockton Convention and Visitors Bureau is nearby. Cruise ships regularly call on Stockton.

On the left bank approaching town you'll pass boat and shipyards. Stockton was an important shipbuilding town during WW II. Today, Stephens Marine builds great yachts, some costing over a million dollars. Colberg's is still active and almost without notice now and then constructs new vessels for San Francisco's Red And White fleet.

You never know what to expect in this area. A submarine moored here for some time just departed. On the south bank you pass the Navy's Rough And Ready Island and there is always a hodgepodge of vessels and amphibians to be seen there. Just above Rough And Ready, the

A sea plane arrives at the Lost Isle docks.

San Joaquin feeds in.

Next is the Port of Stockton, the state's oldest inland port, where you are apt to see ocean-going freighters from Russia and other distant countries loading grain and other cargoes. It can berth 13 steamers at a time and is equipped to handle containerized vessels. The big steamers present no particular hazard to the pleasure boater (you stay out of their way, of course).

It is always a joy to see these behemoths sharing the water with houseboaters. We yell to them and toot horns and they often do the same back. But it was no trifling project getting that deepwater channel dug so that such vessels could ply these waters.

As early as 1874 there were proposals to straighten and deepen the San Joaquin and the channel into Stockton. The river for some 20 miles below Stockton twisted and turned. It was tough for the river boats to negotiate the tight turns. They had colorful names for their favorites, like Turkey Bend and Devil's Elbow.

But regardless of how much the channel was needed, its cost would have been more than any town could afford. Federal support was sought. But it was slow in coming. In 1910 Congress approved funds to widen the lower San Joaquin.

And even that small improvement greatly benefitted shipping.

In 1925 Herbert Hoover, then secretary of commerce, and other Washington officials were given a select cruise of the area by city officials. It was a wonderful ploy. Hoover and his cohorts were greatly impressed with the fertile Delta farmlands. Prior to this, Hoover had taken no stand on the channel project. Now he gave it his support. Stockton had already floated a bond issue to guarantee its portion of the cost.

Varied action on the Channel.

The new Waterfront Yacht Harbor with its Grocers Warehouse building.

It won Congress' approval in 1927. And on February 2, 1933 the channel received its first ship. Most of the Stockton money went to buy right-of-ways. And to this day the Port of Stockton owns many islands along the channel route. There is a move afoot to deepen the channel even more so that larger freighters can be accommodated.

Down river about three miles from the channel head, the Calaveras River feeds in from the east. In Spanish, *calaveras* means skulls. Spanish explorer Moraga gave this name to the river because of skulls he found there. A short distance up the Calaveras is the headquarters of the Stockton Y.C.

Continuing down river you pass the beautiful facilities of the Stockton Sailing Club, then Ladd's Stockton Marina and Stephen's Anchorage (a marina) both in Buckley Cove. Next off on the northeast

bank is Windmill Cove, nearly across from one of two entrances is Fourteen Mile Slough. This slough feeds into modern Village West Marina on the north edge of Stockton, in an area of fine homes and is home of Marina West Y.C.

You can see that even though Stockton fronts on a good deal of water, its marine-oriented businesses are spread out. But the city is their focal point. Still farther down river is 52-acre Lost Isle, then a county boat-in park and picnic grounds on Spud Island. A variety of yacht, water ski and boat clubs occupy some of the islands adjacent to the channel over the next few miles.

Although you would hardly call Stockton "Little Hollywood," movie-making is an important minor activity there. Producers look upon it with favor and many movies and television shows have been filmed there. More than a few of them on

Calamity Jane's in the original Chili Pepper building at the Channel head.

the water.

Just to mention a few, there were "Huck Finn," "All The King's Men," "Blood Alley," "Porgy and Bess," "Cool Hand Luke," and "Bound For Glory." They even filmed "Fat City" there, but hardly by chance. For the book was originally written about Stockton.

John Wayne, Lauren Bacall, Paul Newman, David Carradine, Archie Moore and other stars have acted their parts out around Stockton's Delta. None of them stayed on to become river rats. After all, who'd want to claim Mudville as his home?

Annual events include the Stockton Y.C.'s Decorated Boat Parade in March, the Coors Trans-Delta Hobie-Cat race in May, the Classic Yacht Assn.'s Rendezvous in July and the Marina West Y.C.'s Delta Reflections lighted Christmas boat parade in December.

The Verlon Haile's houseboat decorated for the Marina West Y.C.'s annual lighted boat parade.

T.V. Chan. 3's Weeknight stars, Bette Vasquez and Harry Martin, broadcast live in Stockton aboard John Kamp's houseboat.

The Navy fire boat from Rough & Ready Island leads the parade for the Stockton Y.C.'s annual regatta in March.

The Classic Yacht Association's annual Rendezvous in July at Village West Marina is a fetching event worth seeing.

94

95

THE WATERFRONT
YACHT HARBOR

LOCATED AT THE HEAD OF THE CHANNEL IN DOWNTOWN STOCKTON

The Delta's newest and most spectacular Marina is the focal point of the 100 million dollar Waterfront Redevelopment Project in Downtown Stockton.

Shopping, recreation facilities, and many exciting restaurants are on site. The newly renovated Grocer's Warehouse is a tourist attraction for everyone, and the new Waterfront Promenade leads you right into Downtown Stockton.

The Waterfront Yacht Harbor Offers in a Spotless Setting, a Complete Marina Facility:

- 175 Open and Covered Berths from 30 to 50 Feet in Length.
- The Delta's Largest Guest Dock
- Restroom, Dressing Room, and Showers for Men and Women
- Coin Operated Laundry Facilities
- Regular and Diesel Oil (Mobil, MasterCard, and Visa Credit Cards Welcome)
- Holding Tank Pump Out Facilities
- Security Gates and Roving Security Officers
- Boat Launching Ramp (Within 500 Yards)

The Waterfront Yacht Harbor will be the boater's most popular destination. Why not make it your boat's home while there is still space available?

THE WATERFRONT
YACHT HARBOR

Tuleburg Levee
Stockton, California 95203
(209) 943-1848

SCHMITZ
DEVELOPMENT, INC.
1545 ST MARK'S PLAZA/SUITE ONE
STOCKTON, CA 95207 / 209 477-2671

96

A Chinese freighter makes its way up the Channel toward the Port of Stockton.

Family fun is renting a houseboat. The Stockton area boasts more rental outfits than any other part of the Delta.

A Russian freighter passes the beautiful facilities of the Stockton Sailing Club at Buckley Cove.

12

Picking Wild Berries
By Boat

Delta lore has it that in earlier times a man wanted by the law could slip away into the Delta and live off the land and the water and never be found. When you first look at a Delta map and see its myraid waterways and its hundreds of little islands, it seems as though this could be true. But now that I've boated most every-where on the Delta, I tend to think not.

Ever since farm land reclamation on the Delta gained impetus, there have been a lot of people moving around out there. Any lawman that knew the territory and wanted his man should have been able to hunt him down.

However, a man could *subsist* quite handily out there. There are of course fish and clams and crawdads in plentiful supply. There are plenty of waterfowl. And in earlier times other game was in good supply too.

A man on the run could probably sub-sist on wild blackberries alone through the summer months. This tenacious bush exists along the levee banks through much of the Delta. There seems to be no way to quell it. When a waterway is

dredged and the mud plopped many feet deep on top of the levee blackberry bushes, you figure that's the end of them. But next season they are right there again.

I rather like them. They are nice to have around at breakfast time. And it is not a bad idea to bring cream along when you are cruising during berry season. They go well in pancakes too. With a little Bisquick you can easily make blackberry cobblers.

If you are in the mood to, you can even bake berry pies aboard. One boating writer and his firstmate baked 43 in a season. He weighs 230 pounds! They also espouse canning blackberry jam.

The blackberry season starts by Memorial Day and extends at least into August. In many areas, you can pick them right from the boat. Just nudge the bow into the bushes and start picking. This of course is not advisable along rocky levees that can damage the boat. You can also take the dinghy out for your berry forrays. You can go ashore and pick afoot, but that is not as much in the

Houseboaters pick ber-ries from the bow of their rental boat in The Meadows.

99

spirit of it all.

In my boating gang, you can usually tell the berry pickers by their body scratches. If you are going to be more than a casual berry picker, then you have to come prepared. Bring a long-sleeved shirt, jeans and boots to protect the ankles. Bring a couple pair of tough gloves.

As the season goes on, berries on the outside of the bushes tend to get picked clean. You have to have a means for getting farther into the bush. One boater has a fancy plank he carries aboard for this purpose. It is about 18 inches wide and 5 feet long. It is on a hinge arrangement that lets him double the length. He keeps one end of the plank on the boat and drops the rest of it atop the berry bushes. When he steps onto it, it settles in

but supports his weight quite handily.

You can also use a big piece of carpet for this purpose. Just spread it out on the offending brambles, then climb on it to pick farther into the bush. The real organizers bring hedge shears so they can cut a path into the berry supply.

Several of the little plastic buckets you buy for about a quarter in paint stores work out fine. You'll need a bigger container on the boat for dumping the pails in. Some pickers clip the pails to their belt to free both hands. If you do this, dump your pail when it is half full to avoid spillage. You wear the glove on your left hand only and hold the branch with it, picking with your right hand. Excess berries not eaten can be bagged and frozen, to be enjoyed later in the year.

13

Bethel Island— Hub Of The Delta

Bethel Island's importance to the boating community goes unquestioned. It is the boating capitol of the Delta, and no one makes any bones about it. Nearly 100 businesses are located on or near this 3,554-acre levee-protected island. And virtually every one of them would be in dire straits if it were not for the boating market.

Looking at it the other way, the boater is mighty lucky to have such a concentration of marine supplies, facilities and support services at his disposal. And most Delta boaters make at least one annual pilgrimage there to avail themselves of this marine smorgasbord.

It represents easy shopping for anyone in search of a boat, new or used. I would estimate that within 200 yards of the only bridge to the island, over a dozen different makes of new boats can be purchased. And they represent some of the best marques to be had. Most are in stock and in the water. Anyone who has traipsed all over the countryside shopping for boats can appreciate this.

All the rest of the good stuff is there too. Marine chandleries, prop repair, engine mechanics, outdrive specialists, marine surveyors and insurance brokers who speak boat talk. You can get your marine radio fixed, buy an island through a real estate broker and rent anything from a luxurious houseboat to a funky little fishing skiff—all at Bethel Island.

The island is ringed with marinas and covered berthing and private docks with comfortable homes and weekend getaways poking up over the levees. Estimates have the boat count there in the order of 2,000. There are campgrounds and mobile home parks on the island, the latter of which support a growing retirement community. Three yacht clubs call Bethel Island home, the busiest of which is the San Joaquin Y.C. with its clubhouse on a barge on pilings off to the right as you cross the bridge.

Everything on Bethel Island is referenced from the bridge.

The new two-lane high-clearance bridge came after WW II when recreation boaters began to discover this sleepy little island. Before that, Bethel made-do quite nicely with a single-lane wooden bridge. For years it had been a farming island like so many others in the Delta. Asparagus, sugar beets, corn, barley, celery, beans, onions and other crops thrived there.

In the levee-building days, Bethel had been part of a large holding that included Franks and Webb tracts and Bradford and Jersey islands. As early as 1885 there

The active Bethel Water Ski Club performs.

were Bethels listed as part owners. Its name sometimes changed with new owners and it was known as Stone's Tract and Sandmound Ranch. It is said that the island eventually came under the ownership of a Major W. K. Bethell. Although that spelling seems confusing.

When Jack and Blanche Farrar cleared an eucalyptus grove near the bridge to make a picnic area in the 1920s, it was the first recreational enterprise on the island. How things have changed. Farrar Park is still there, but now as a thriving marina and boat yard. Farming dwindled as boating took over.

Bethel Island's location is handy and boaters can leave there for a variety of destinations in many directions. *Victory II*, a handsome free-running diesel ferry shuttles autos from neighboring Jersey Island to Webb Tract and Bradford Island. When a temporary rock dam was installed across Dutch Slough to Jersey Island because of the drought in 1977, island farmers complained that they began to see coyotes on their land!

The actual town of Bethel Island is but a few blocks off Bethel Island Road just over the bridge. It has a post office and is sprinkled with a few stores, shops, bars and restaurants. Except on summer weekends when the weekend warriors are out in force, it is *still* a sleepy town. Most of the residents hail from somewhere else. And they came to Bethel Island because they like its rural charm.

Things are sure to change in the future. An up-to-date sewer system is now in operation, and some very exciting development projects are now on the drawing boards. One includes breaching the levee to form an inner lagoon with waterfront homes and businesses. The sleeping giant is being awakened.

Dog days boating at Bethel Island.

Some boaters are aggravated by the interminal 5 mph zones around much of the island because of the berthed boats. But I personally rather enjoy poking along past the berthed boats. You get to rubberneck. You find out what's for sale. And you get to have a look at the hokey names some owners bestow upon their boats.

Bethel Island has a potpourri of annual events that include the Frozen Bun Run for waterskiers New Year's morning, a gala Opening Day decorated boat parade sponsored by the San Joaquin Y.C. in April and a Thanksgiving week Fall Fishing Derby sponsored by the Chamber of Commerce.

Some of the filming for the movie "Huckleberry Finn" took place near Franks Tract back in 1959. It included a scene of a paddlewheeler rounding the bend in the early morning light. The directors liked the tranquilty of the area. They ought to stop by for a look on say a weekend in July!

An intrepid water skier leaps off the Bethel Island bridge to come up water skiing— barefoot!

Above. Antics at the Jan. 1 Frozen Bun Run. R., top to bottom. The San Joaquin Y.C. April opener parade starts the season. Bottom. Fishing on Dutch Slough. Below. The S.F. to Disco Bay row-in stops at Carol's Harbor.

14

Franks Tract Lake

Franks Tract, often called a "submerged lake", is about the same size as Bethel Island and is situated between it and the San Joaquin River. Originally reclaimed in 1902, it was merely another Delta island given over to farming until that fateful day in the winter of 1937 when the False River levee crumbled and the tract was inundated.

The tract's reclamation district assessed itself $100,000 to repair the levee and pump the island dry. Barely had this work been accomplished by late 1938 when the levee again broke. But alas, by then funds had been exhausted and owners had no choice but to let the tract remain a vast lake. One owner though, Fred Franks (whose father the tract had been named after) reclaimed his 400-acre parcel, making a cut to separate it from the main tract. This partially submerged acreage today is maintained as a natural wildlife preserve on the northeast corner of the tract by the State Parks Department and is referred to as "Little Franks Tract".

Although it is known that the waters of Franks Tract hide old tractors, fence posts, remains of farm buildings, tree stumps, utility pole stubs and more, knowing boaters use the tract as a short cut to other places, for water skiing, fishing and just plain cruising. It has never been properly mapped by the N.O.A.A., and many rental houseboat operators designate it as off limits for their boats.

To enter the tract, you must find one of the sufficiently deep openings over the old levees. These same levees provide many excellent anchorages, some with quite-fetching sandy low-tide beaches. The entire tract is now a State Recreation Area (no hunting allowed).

Franks Tract has long been a prime striped bass fishing area, for the fish are attracted to its relatively warm waters. After WW II a community of modest fishing resorts blossomed on neighboring Bethel Island. During its heyday, as many as 500 rental fishing boats were available

It was on these pilings at the entrance of Franks Tract that a little shack rested. From there the toll collector charged each who entered the Tract.

Some of the old levees that ring Franks Tract now make excellent anchorages (on windless days) with low-tide sandy beaches.

there, typically renting for $1.50 per day. Resort owners would tow long strings of the boats, anglers and gear aboard, out to the tract to anchor. Then they would return for them in the late afternoon. In those days, few anglers owned their own outboard motors.

Circle Fishing

The tract even spawned its own fishing methods. One was called "circle fishing", in which anglers would gather to form a large circle with their anchored boats to sort of keep the feeding stripers confined inside the circle. It is said that you could walk from boat to boat in those tight circles. There were more than a few altercations between anglers who would tangle lines and even both try to drag in the same fish. More sophisticated anglers considered circle fishing most unsportsmanlike.

Another method was "half-dollar fishing". After casting out, the angler would strip off from 15 to 30 feet of extra line and lay it in a coil on the boat seat. To keep it in place, a half-dollar was placed on the coil. As a striper began toying with the bait, it would gently pull line from the coil. No matter how excited he might be, the angler would do nothing at this stage. Only after the striper had pulled all the line from the coil was it time to set the hook.

With hundreds of fishmen gathered out on the tract, there was obviously room for entreprenuers. One was the "good humor man" who outfitted a little pontoon boat with supplies such as hot coffee, donuts, sandwiches and other items. He would thread his way through the assemblage of boats on the tract, purveying his goods.

The Power Poles

PG&E had a conventional power line across Franks Tract dating to about 1908. After the inundation, the submerged poles were replaced with 45 and 50-foot poles. In 1943 these were replaced with 35-foot pilings onto which 35-foot poles were spliced. There were hassles and even law suits with yachtsmen who would catch radio antennas, masts and other boat parts on the lines. In 1948 the pilings were replaced with new ones 10 feet longer. PG&E was striving for a minimum high-tide clearance of 25 feet.

One power line went from Webb Tract to Holland Tract and was referred to by boaters as "the long pole line". Another, called "the short pole line" came from Quimby Island and intersected with this line. In 1958 PG&E removed the lines and replaced them with the present high-clearance lines that effectively circumvent the tract. Divers were hired to cut off the pilings one foot from the bottom. Another nostalgic landmark gone.

For several years during the fifties, the Navy had a practice bombing range on the tract. "The Navy used to hire me to tow the targets out," remembers Frank Andronico of Franks Resort. Even though the bombers used harmless smoke bombs, it was to say the least unsettling for fishermen on the tract to look up to see a bomber bearing down on them!

Toll Gates

Some time after inundation of the tract, it was purchased by several enterprising fellows who had a scheme for profiting from the tract's popularity with anglers. They drove in pilings and placed barges to block off its various entrances, leaving but a single opening, located on Piper Slough. There they constructed a toll gate shack on pilings. A toll collector sat in the shack and demanded a 50-cent toll from each boat entering the tract.

To say the least, the scheme met with hostility. There was much shaking of fists and waving of shotguns. Finally, after a four-year battle by recreation angling interests, on January 30, 1952 the State Supreme Court ruled the tract was a navigable portion of the San Joaquin River and therefore open to the public for free fishing.

The Parks Department started purchase of Franks Tract and Little Franks Tract in 1959. It consisted of 13 separate parcels with ten owners. Final acquisition took place in 1975. Popularity of this "submerged lake" continues, although few boaters care to be out on it on a windy day when there are whitecaps of considerable proportions.

Close ties exist between Bethel Island and Franks Tract. The majority of boaters who use the tract keep boats at, or launch at, Bethel Island. The convenience is obvious. And when the stripers are in, Bethel Islanders only need to take a few minutes to go to the tract for a limit.

15

Locke & Walnut Grove—
Historic River Towns

Locke and Walnut Grove are a comfortable pair of old river towns that I never tire of visiting. Roaming their streets and back alleys lined with tired old clapboard buildings is like exploring another world. There is the decided feel of the early western town to both places. And you half expect to see gunslingers squaring off out in front of the saloon on Main Street.

Although both towns front on the water and in fact are nearly surrounded by water, they are not overwhelmed by boating activity. They retain their heritage, wearing the cloak of history quite well. The bistros and shops are populated more by farmers and grain buyers and produce haulers than by boaters. And this makes a visit all the more enjoyable.

Boating access to Walnut Grove is easy and convenient thanks to the fine merchants dock on the Sacramento just below the bridge at the juncture of Georgiana Slough. This is said to be the first bascule bridge built west of the Mississippi. From the guest dock, you merely trundle over the levee and Walnut Grove is spread out before you, although not exactly majestically so I'm afraid.

But getting into Locke by boat is a trifle more complicated. I've boated in behind Locke on Dredger Cut and tied to the tree limbs. Then trudged over the railroad bed and braved attack from ferocious dogs to get to Locke the back way. But I can hardly recommend this practice, since I had the distinct feeling I was trespassing while doing so (besides, the dogs appeared meaner each time). A better choice is to secure to the Walnut Grove docks and make the hike of less than a mile.

Sometimes you can cadge a ride from some of the marina folk at Wimpy's or

Walnut Grove Marina and sometimes dock boys will drive you over for a fee. But this practice is not very consistent.

The Cross Delta gates will not clear most houseboats and cruisers, so you cannot easily get into the Sacramento from the Meadows area.

Fortunately, The Boathouse in Locke, fronting on the Sacramento, has recently installed a good guest dock and there is a fee for leaving your boat there for three hours while exploring Locke. Boathouse also has fuel, dry boat storage, launching, and some marine supplies. There is a grocery store in Locke.

There are those who might object to a guest-dock tie-up fee, but docks come expensive these days and Boathouse does not have a great many revenue-producing activities. It represents a convenient way into Locke and prices aren't out of line. And those of us not over-fond of ankle-biting dogs or long hikes gladly pay our dock fees.

Actually, the Boathouse pre-dates Locke itself. It was another of the riverside produce storage sheds that once dotted the Delta waterways. The first portion of the building was constructed in the late 1890's, and the remainder was completed in 1921. Both riverboats and trains of the Southern Pacific railroad could pull right up to its doors. To obtain information on docking here, call (916) 776-1204.

Locke is unique in that it is the only rural Chinese community existing in the country. It is listed in the National Register of Historic Places. And there is legislation afoot (to the tune of over $3 million) to purchase the town property and transform Locke into a living monument.

None of the Chinese presently living there would be displaced. The ramshackle two-story buildings would be left

Locke's old Star Theatre

looking pretty much as they are now. Although a new sewer system would be installed, propane heat and cooking stoves would go, and the buildings would be rewired for all-electric to lessen fire hazards. The transformation would take place slowly over a 10-year period.

Locke is not as old as its weathered buildings would suggest. The first town building was erected by Tin Sin Chan in 1912 and he is generally credited as the town's founder. The building was a saloon. A boarding house and gambling hall followed. Then a fire destroyed the Chinese section of Walnut Grove in 1915.

Members of the Yeung Wong Tong elected not to rebuild in Walnut Grove. Under the guidance of Lee Bing, a half dozen families obtained permission from sympathetic rancher George Locke to begin a new town where one of his pear orchards stood. Six 2-story $1200 structures soon rose. They were built against the land side of the levee, with the top story fronting on the levee road and with the back on the main street below the levee—just as they stand today.

The structures were not unlike those built by the pioneers a half century earlier. They were butted together with only occasional alley space to allow outside access to the street below. There were hitching posts, and balconies leaned out over the creaking board walks, providing respite from the hot noon-day sun.

The harsh Alien Land Law at the time prevented Chinese from owning land. The builders apparently trusted George Locke, for they proceeded with only a verbal lease. And on that a town was built. Even today, Locke homeowners do not own the property their homes rest on.

The town was known as Lockeport and it began to grow. By 1920 the name had been shortened to Locke. Prohibition came and Locke flourished. There were gambling halls, bordellos, opium dens and booze joints. Daily bus service connected Locke with other Chinese villages and with San Francisco.

On their day off, field workers from the surrounding territory were brought to Locke so they could have a good time and relieve some of the tensions pent up from their regimen of hard labor in the fields.

At one time Locke had a permanent population of some 400, that seasonally swelled to 1500. But time has since taken its toll. The younger generation of Chinese left Locke for more opportune places. To make their fortunes elsewhere. Today only a handful of Chinese and other Asians call Locke home. A few Caucasians have moved in, some to open businesses in town. At times, it seems as though Al-The-Wop's has more customers than Locke has residents.

Preservation of Locke could be a worth-

Walnut Grove is just over the levee.

113

while undertaking as long as the town is not transformed into a tourist trap. There is a certain honesty to the place now. It would not be the same without uneven board walks and washing flapping in the gentle breeze blowing across the high balconies. Without water sitting in the pot holes on the back streets and home owners tending their tiny vegetable gardens.

Yet the Chinese do deserve a monument. But it should not be at the expense of their way of life for the few old timers remaining. The Chinese played a vitally important role in reclamation of the Delta. And the Delta has long been well known back in China. Consider that the Chinese came to California to work on the transcontinental railroad, but they did so for no more than 5 years. Yet they toiled on the Delta levees and in the fields for over a half century. And tales of the Delta were carried back to China.

Lin Sen, a Chinese who lived in the river town of Courtland for awhile, returned to his homeland and became president of the Republic of China. And it is said that it was the Chinese who introduced Californians to the salad. Food that early Delta ranchers thought fit only for the livestock!

At one time there were many settlements similar to Locke around the Delta. But they have all disappeared. We boaters are fortunate that Locke remains for our enjoyment in a simple and uncomplicated way. There is only one Locke.

Walnut Grove

Neighboring Walnut Grove was founded in 1851 by John Sharp and he was instrumental in development of the area. He ran a ferry across the river and this played an important part in Walnut Grove developing on both sides of the river. It is the only river town south of Red Bluff that occupies both sides of the Sacramento.

By 1865 there was a busy saw mill in Walnut Grove that helped provide lumber to a Delta that was fast a-growing. When Sharp died in 1880, his widow sold their property to a Mrs. Agnes Brown who with her son Alex operated a hotel there. The town bank that he founded still bears his name and it is said that he was the first one to plant asparagus in the Delta.

Walnut Grove prospered as a produce shipping point on the route of the paddlewheelers. When the more daring riverboat skippers on the Sacramento-San Francisco run began taking their chances with the snags on Steamboat Slough for the great shortcut it provided, stops at Walnut Grove lessened somewhat. There was still plenty of waterfront activity there, however. It was a natural stop on the Sacramento-Stockton run via Georgiana Slough, as it remains even today for the pleasure boat fleet.

The Chinese quarter of Walnut Grove burned in 1915 and again in 1937. But the Chinese influence lingers still in the town. A string of business establishments are entrenched atop the levee. Some of the old buildings have been renovated into very attractive structures.

Behind the levee though is a weathered old town not unlike Locke. The wooden clapboard buildings with peeling paint and faint lettering from old business signs here too lend the feel of an early western cow town. And in fact western movies have been filmed here.

On the opposite bank of the Sacramento is Deckhands Marine with supplies and a guest dock. Behind the levee is an attractive residential section of Walnut Grove that few boaters know exists.

Walnut Grove and Locke are handily separated by the Cross Delta Channel. And from the channel's shore rises the tallest structure in the state. It is a tower poking 1,549 feet skyward, supporting 4 television antennas. One cool spring day Joanie and I shoehorned ourselves into the tower's cubical of an elevator with engineer Bill Barclay for the 18 minute ride up the center of the tower to the top. Up there, where the air is clean and the winds blow briskly, there is a platform the size of city building lot and it is remarkably stable.

We were lucky, for there are no such rides for the general public. At the entrance to the tower road by the channel there is a sign with some interesting statistics on the tower. It is worth stopping to read during your walk to Locke.

These two old river towns like boaters. And boaters in turn appreciate the towns. Who could ask for more?

115

116

16

Rio Vista—
On The Sacramento River

Rio Vista (or Rio Visty, as oldtimers were prone to call it) is an amiable Delta river town situated on the banks of a broad section of the Sacramento River. Ocean-going freighters bound for the port of Sacramento cruise by it and under its busy tower draw bridge.

Founded in 1857 by Colonel N. H. Davis, the town was originally located a couple miles above the bridge near Cache Slough. After its buildings were wiped out by a flood a few years later, it was moved to its present, more amiable, site. In later years, it boasted the world's largest asparagus cannery. But a crop blight spelled its demise.

Rio Vista is credited with staging California's first bass fishing derby back in 1933. To this day it is a razzle dazzle affair attracting fishermen from near and far. In fish size, it has come a long way. The 1933 winner was a mere 8 pounder, while in 1973 the winner tipped the scales at 55 pounds.

The derby festivities take place annually in October. There is a carnival with rides with many local booths purveying food and other goodies. The town spills over for this. And I wouldn't miss it for anything.

Fishing in the Rio Vista area is excellent. And the little town boasts a passle of fine bait shops. In 1974 crawdad racing was added as a bass derby competition. Very apropos, since one of the Delta's most prominent crawdad suppliers is located in the city.

Lifestyle in Rio Vista is casual and peaceful. Tucked away in the quietude of its streets you'll find many splendid proud old homes of Victorian style. This gives hint that there has been, and probably

Bill Stratton's 390-lb. sturgeon.

Winning striper in 1981 Derby.

still is, money here. In the mid-1930's huge natural gas fields were discovered nearby, making lucky farmers instantly wealthy.

Several dredging outfits are based out of Rio Vista and you see their huge dredges tied along the waterfront docks. It was these and others like them that made reclamation of the Delta possible. Some of them are almost like little hotels. They have a fulltime cook aboard. The crews work, eat and sleep aboard, sometimes not going back home for weeks on end.

Down river from the town at St. Joseph's Cut is the full-service Delta Marina with Walton's boat yard with haulout and the Point restaurant out front. In days past, this cut was indeed a busy place. Farmers would moor barges and boats of all descriptions there, transporting sheep, cattle and work horses to the many Delta islands. Later, the cut became a little enclave for houseboaters who paid $1.50 per month rent to the firm that managed the property. Farther down river the Coast Guard maintains a large station and barracks facility that covers all of the Delta and more.

Rio Vista has some prominence as a shipping port and was port-of-call for many of the old paddlewheelers. The Paddlewheeler *Yosemite* exploded there at great loss of life. The steamers used to tie up in town near what is now Main Street. And the water was often deep enough for small boats to anchor all the way up to Front Street.

There is limited docking at the municipal dock where you can tie up to shop in town or perhaps stop for a meal or libation. The shopping area is well concentrated and has about everything you might need. Overnight tie up can sometimes be arranged, but check in ahead of time at the court house. Most houseboaters prefer to stay out at Delta Marina.

There is a municipal launching ramp in town for trailerboaters. And a new campground and RV park with launching was recently built in the dunes area down river from town.

The Sacramento is close to 1,000 feet wide in the Rio Vista area and winds sweeping in off the Montezuma Hills can raise a good chop. Sailboaters aren't a bit adverse to this, but houseboaters need to use some care here when the winds are blowing hard.

Rio Vista is Spanish for River View. A name I think you'll agree is appropriate.

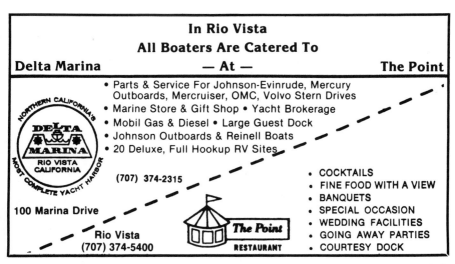

Above. Guest dock at Delta Marina. Above R. Derby weigh-in time. Below. Nice boat passes Outrigger Marina. R. & R. below. The Rio Vista Parade always has much variety.

17

Courtland to Sacramento

A cruise up the Sacramento River from the hamlet of Courtland to the capital city is not fraught with that feel of discovery found in many other Delta cruises. For once underway, the choice of alternate routes is nil. The last navigable slough jutting off was Sutter Slough below Courtland. And now there's only you and the meandering river.

But you are traveling up the waters of history, where the paddlewheelers and sailing scows and the 49ers have passed before you. And the once-bustling little river towns along the route even today are worth your attention. There is a string of marinas en route, some with plenty of character—and some populated by characters. Water depth is good, the route is marked and the dreaded wing dams have been removed. The Sacramento is a strong river, however, and during spring runoffs the current can be more swift than you would believe.

Courtland is one of my favorite Sacramento River towns. And it is situated smack in the heart of pear country. Each year its festive Pear-Fair takes place the last Sunday in July with a parade, a carnival, games, art shows and a good many activities that include pears. The big competition is among the farmers to see who has grown the largest pear. And the winners weigh in at several pounds.

The town was founded in 1870 by James Sims, a native of England who had come to California from Canada and finally tired of seeking his fortune in the gold mines. Courtland historically had a large Chinese population and their houses, high up on stilts, crowded the river front. Existence for them was perilous and the China Towns were often devastated by flood and fire.

Courtland Docks is a pleasant stop here, with a long overnight guest dock, a good restaurant and rental houseboats. Just across the levee you'll find a good market, a drug store, a post office and even a library.

The next river town is Hood, a sleepy

Courtland Docks provides convenient access to this river hamlet.

farming community that was established in 1909 and named after William Hood, a construction engineer with the old Sacramento Southern Railroad. Plans were to re-route the railroad's main line that then ran from Suisun to make it run along the Sacramento River and then connect in with the main line out of Antioch. But the scheme never saw fruition and the line eventually was completed only as far as Isleton.

Even this line has now been abandoned. There is talk of running an excursion train from Sacramento over these tracks to connect with an excursion boat for round trips. And maybe someday it will happen. There are no public boat landings at Hood. But perhaps completion of the new Interstate 5 which now passes nearby might revitalize the town and encourage someone to install docks and other facilities.

It is here at Hood that the big 43-mile ditch for the proposed Peripheral Canal would depart. The canal would be capable of draining off 80 percent of the Sacramento River's flow and would include a fish screen that could be up to two miles long. Dept. of Fish and Game has been operating a test fish screen at Hood for several years.

Clarksburg & Freeport

Next you pass Clarksburg, off on the west bank. Clarksburg Landing here has a guest dock and sling launching, but little more. Across the levee is a good old-fashioned general store that is a joy to browse in. In town is another store and a residential community that could be a model for a movie of a quiet farming town.

The town was settled in 1849 by Judge Robert Clark and in its early days had a heavy Portuguese population. Later, much of the land in the area was purchased by the Netherlands Farming Company. By then, many settlers had arrived from the Netherlands, introducing that country's levee-building techniques. In its tender years, Clarksburg suffered many devastating floods. On some Delta maps, Elk Slough appears to connect with the Sacramento here, but there is no access. Anyway, Elk Slough is shallow and snag ridden and not much used by boatmen these days. A couple miles below Clarks-

burg is a public fishing access with room for a few RVs and a free launching ramp.

Continuing up river, off on the east bank is Cliff's Marina, with a guest dock, fuel, berthing, snack bar and other supplies. Next, just past a great bascule drawbridge, is Freeport Marina, probably the most modern and complete facility on this cruise. It has covered berthing, guest docking, fuel and plenty of other supplies. Across the street is a cafe.

In the waning days of the gold rush, the town of Freeport was an important shipping center for the mines. Freeport was founded in 1862 by the Freeport Railroad Company in an effort to avoid a hefty tax the city of Sacramento levied on all passengers and freight that left the river to connect with the railroad. By moving the rail center to Freeport, Sacramento was effectively bypassed and the new town was indeed literally a "free port". Too, there is a big bend in the river above Freeport that was a bane to sailing vessels that sometimes had to lay over for several days waiting for the proper wind.

A. J. Bump's is a saloon and restaurant in Freeport that dates back to 1863 when it was established as a general store. The food is good and this is an active and interesting place to visit. It is about a quarter-mile trek up from the marina and guest docking arrangements can be made.

Sacramento Area

Cruising up river from here, you are hardly aware of the residential tangle that

There's no shortage of launching facilities

spreads out from Sacramento on the east bank, growing ever closer to Freeport. But the west bank, even behind the levee, retains its rural flavor.

Public launching facilities are many and good in the Sacramento area. But the boatman with a big cruiser has to carefully choose his destinations. There is surely no surfeit of guest docking for large craft. Up from Freeport, you first pass Light 29 Marina with guest docking, a beer bar and some supplies. Next is the fine public launching facility at Garcia Bend, then Garcia Bend Marina with but few facilities. Over on the west bank then is Four Seasons Marina with a hodgepodge of interesting craft at its roomy dock. This is a good operation, with an active beer bar, good guest docking, a cafe, easy fuel dock and diesel and other supplies.

Then on the opposite bank there's the Pilot House (formerly Da Rosa Marina) a small marina. It has a bar and snacks.

Then back to the west bank is Sherwood Harbor, a jumping little place that manages to stuff a surprising number of fun lovers into its floating digs. Just above this is the splendid new clubhouse of the active Sacramento Yacht Club, maybe the oldest yacht club in the Delta. Across the river is Captain's Table Marina, which once accommodated a fine floating restaurant popular with boatmen. But it burned a few years ago and was never replaced. Only the marina remains. Plans are afoot to build a new restaurant ashore.

On the edge of Sacramento you'll find the Sacramento Boat Harbor, a fine city-run marina at Miller Park with fuel, guest docking and free launching. Just opposite the Sacramento Ship Channel there is a small float where you can tie to walk up to a surprisingly well-stocked snack bar in the park.

You'll pass within a stone's throw of Old Sacramento, a splendidly renovated section of the city with many restaurants and shops. But alas, there is not the hint of a boating facility and no practical way you can get ashore. There is much talk of developing the waterfront here and some of the plans call for guest docking. It is direly needed, but perhaps may be a long way off. The master plan even calls for a 400-passenger paddlewheeler to shuttle passengers into Old Sacramento.

Interesting.

On the left bank, in Broderick, Tom Raley (of Raley's Drug Stores) has renovated the old Marina Inn motel and designated the site as Raley's Landing. And a plaque registers it as the site of the first Pacific Coast salmon cannery. You can overnight in the motel, dine at its Wheelhouse Restaurant, or brunch (Sundays only) or have parties at the outdoors Inn Tent. There's limited guest docking, by advance reservation only. Small boats can tie to the bank and get ashore here. It's about an eight-minute trek to Old Sacramento from here. Each year Old Sacramento has its four-day Dixieland Jazz Jubliee, the largest in the world, over Memorial Day weekend. It is a wonderful event.

In the paddlewheelers' heyday, many of the proud old vessels were at docks or on ways for repairs or construcion at Broderick. It was important to Sacramento. And it was a terrible night on August 28, 1932 when fire struck a fleet of steamboats anchored here. Sacramento's fire department answered the alarm, but halted at the river. For Broderick is not only outside the Sacramento City limits, but it is also outside Sacramento County.

Valiant tugboat captains managed to pull a few vessels clear of the inferno. But by the time the ashes had settled, at least eight fine old steamboats could be counted as destroyed, plus numerous other craft. One of the first to go was the paddlewheeler *Flora*, which you may have seen as *Dixie* in the movie *Huckleberry Finn*. Another was *San Joaquin No. 4*, once considered the most powerful inland vessel in America. This was a sad night for those who dearly loved the old paddlewheelers.

Today, the scenario is different at Broderick, although there still is a variety of watercraft snugged to its banks. You'll find a fine public launching facility, then the Chart Room Marina, an active floating facilitiy. You can get food and libations here and plenty of lively conversation. Next is quiet Viewpoint Marina with berthing and a neighboring boat yard. Then comes floating River Galley, the most popular boat-in restaurant in the area. Across the river from it is Discovery Park, with a fine public launch. The American

River swings off to the starboard and there are some good anchorages to its left bank up against the park.

Bridges on the Sacramento have good clearance and are well tended. The I Street bridge, near here, is interesting in that it accommodates both train and auto traffic. In fact, it has two sets of train tracks. I can recall being aboard the 125 ft. Sea Scout vessel *Alert*, waiting for this bridge to open while two Amtrak trains were crossing over it in opposite directions.

If you continue up the Sacramento, you'll find Village Marina with dining and cocktails and limited docking, then Crawdad's River Saloon (formerly B & B Marina) presently with no docking. The nearby Virgin Sturgeon, once a floating bistro favored by Governor Jerry Brown, has been done in by the ravages of fire and sinking and is no more. Next up is River View Marina, all brand new with deluxe covered berthing, roomy guest docking, a snack bar and various supplies.

The American River is popular with small boats and sees plenty of traffic. But its swift waters are shallow and offer little for skippers of large craft. In fact, all this lower portion of the American has been zoned 5 mph.

Sacramento Ship Channel

Skippers heading to Sacramento from anywhere in the Rio Vista area might do well to consider using the Sacramento Ship Channel via Cache Slough, which clips 16 miles off the river route. The Channel, which was dug in 1963 to give freighters easy passage to the Port of Sacramento, has almost no perceptible current. Thus it can be both a time and fuel saver on a Sacramento cruise. But this run is strictly dullsville. Scenery is nil. There are no marinas, fuel stops or anything else on the route. If you are lucky, you might see a passing freighter. Dull or not, heading to Sacramento via the Channel and returning via the river (with maybe a six knot current helping) makes a practical cruise.

The Sacramento Lock (officially the William G. Stone Lock) connects the river with the Channel. It is 600 ft. long and 86 ft. wide and is touted as the only navigational lock in the state (actually, I believe there is also a private lock somewhere in California). Its use is free and Delta boatmen might want to try it once just for the experience.

Water levels between the Sacramento and the Channel can vary as much as 21 ft. and on rare occasions, such as during a drought year, the river can be as much as 2½ ft. below the Channel. About four to six times a year the levels are equal. When the difference is little, locking through is a piece of cake. But when the difference is great, as during spring runoffs, with a water wall of close to 20 ft. rushing in from the Sacramento when the gates are opened, it can be both an exciting and maybe perilous experience. Then you best have the boat well fendered and have the crew at ready with boat hooks.

River View Marina is a full-service new marina in the Sacramento area, just above the American River.

Unfortunately, the Army Corps of Engineers has elected to discontinue operation of the lock, deeming it too expensive for the use it receives. Corps operation will cease September 30, 1982. Operation till then is on a curtailed schedule: Monday, Thursday and Friday, 8 a.m. to 4 p.m.; Tuesday and Wednesday closed; Saturday and Sunday 7 a.m. to 7 p.m.; closed holidays except Memorial Day, Independence Day and Labor Day, operating 7 a.m. to 7 p.m. It will operate Tuesdays following Monday holidays, 8 a.m. to 4 p.m.

There is a drawbridge on the Channel side which will not open during the weekday commute hours of 7 to 9 a.m. and 4 to 6 p.m. Depending on tide, clearance is usually 13 to 20 feet. Normally you lock to the river on the half hour (try to arrive a little early) and to the Channel on the hour. Both VHF channels 16 and nine are monitored, with nine as the talk channel.

You signal the lock with two long and two short blasts of the boat horn about a half mile before entrance. There are marked "talk stations" on each end where you can talk to the lock tender over a P.A. system. But at the river end, the tender can't actually see you at the station. If there is much noise around, he may not hear your horn signal and you'll need to use the talk station. There are red, yellow and green visual signals for lock entry. Sound signals from the tender include one long to enter the lock, one short to leave the lock and four shorts for stand clear or emergency stop. You tie your boat to the floating mooring bits on the lock wall.

Passage reads more complicated than it really is. I entered the lock with trepidations my first time, but was through it before I realized anything was happening. If you want to ponder the procedure from the comforts of your living room, you can obtain a free brochure on the lock by writing the U.S. Army Corps of Engineers, 650 Capitol Mall, Sacramento, CA 95814. The lockmaster's phone number is (916) 371-7540. When you clear the lock up river, Miller Park lies dead ahead.

Note: A local task force is proposing local operation of the lock. And at this writing proposals are being reviewed by those in authority. Information on future operation of the lock may be obtained from Tel. (916) 440-2326.

Above. Old Chinese building in Courtland. Above, R. Old Sacramento Dixieland Jazz Jubilee. R. Decorated boat at Sacramento Y.C. parade. Below, R. New guest dock at Raley's Landing.

127

128

ADVERTISER INDEX

129

Where To Rent A Houseboat
Phone Or Write For Free Brochure

Herman & Helen's Houseboats
Venice Island Ferry
Stockton, CA 95209
Tel. (209) 951-4634

Recreation Rentals
P.O. Box 2182
Petaluma, CA 94953
Tel. (707) 762-2438

Delta Country Houseboats
P.O. Box 246
Walnut Grove, CA 95690
Tel. (916) 776-1741

Courtland Docks Houseboats
P.O. Box 427
Courtland, CA 95615
Tel. (916) 775-1360

Lazy Days Houseboats Rentals
P.O. Box 819
Bethel Island, CA 94511
Tel. (415) 684-3641

Take Five Charters
P.O. Box 6339
Stockton, CA 95206
Tel. (209) 948-1712

New Hope Landing
W. Walnut Grove Road
P.O. Box 417
Thornton, CA 95686
Tel. (209) 794-2627

Delta Van Cruiser
950 Marina Circle
Suisun, CA 94585
Tel. (707) 427-0206

Islander Cruises
P.O. Box 1191
Boulder Creek, CA 95006
Tel. (408) 243-5400

Delta Van Cruiser
Rt. 2, Box 402
3255 Wells Road
Oakley, CA 94561
Tel. (415) 684-2770

Holiday Flotels, Delta
11540 W. Eight Mile Rd.
Stockton, CA 95209
Tel. (209) 477-9544

S & H Boat Yard
Box 514
Antioch, CA 94509
Tel. (415) 757-3621

Paradise Point Marina
8095 N. Rio Blanco Road
Stockton, CA 95209
Tel. (209) 952-1000

King Island Houseboats
11530 W. Eight Mile Rd.
Stockton, CA 95209
Tel. (209) 478-0210

Camp-A-Float (for RVs)
Venice Island Ferry
Stockton, CA 95209
Tel. (209) 951-4634

Delta Adventures
P.O. Box 607
3955 Willow Road
Bethel Island, CA 94511
Tel. (415) 684-2884

Delta Area Chambers of Commerce

Antioch Chamber of Commerce
212 'H' St., Antioch, CA 94509
Tel. (415) 757-1800

Benicia Chamber of Commerce
P.O. Box 185, Benicia, CA 94510
Tel. (707) 745-2120

Bethel Island Chamber of Commerce
P.O. Box 263, Bethel, Island, CA 94511
Tel. (415) 684-3220

Delta Chambers, Inc.
1105 N. El Dorado, Stockton, CA 95202
Tel. (209) 466-7066

Isleton Chamber of Commerce
P.O. Box 758, Isleton, CA 95641
Tel. (916) 777-6082

Lodi Chamber of Commerce
P.O. Box 386, Lodi, CA 95241
Tel. (209) 334-4773

Martinez Chamber of Commerce
620 Las Juntas, Martinez, CA 94553
Tel. (415) 228-2345

Pittsburg Chamber of Commerce
2010 Railroad Ave., Pittsburg, CA 94565
Tel. (415) 432-7301

Rio Vista Chamber of Commerce
60 Main St., Rio Vista, CA 94571
Tel. (707) 374-2700

Stockton Chamber of Commerce
1105 N. El Dorado, Stockton, CA 95202
Tel. (209) 466-7066

Stockton Convention & Visitors Bureau
46 W. Fremont St., Stockton, CA 95202
Tel. (209) 943-1987

Tracy Chamber of Commerce
P.O. Box 891, Tracy, CA 95376
Tel. (209) 835-2131